A Witch's

Beverages
and Brews

Magick Potions Made Easy

By
Patricia Telesco

NEW PAGE BOOKS
A division of The Career Press, Inc.
Franklin Lakes, NJ

A WITCH'S BEVERAGES AND BREWS
Cover design by Cheryl Finbow
Illustrated by Colleen Koziara
Typesetting by Eileen Munson
Printed in the U.S.A. by Book-mart Press

To order this title, please call toll-free 1-800-CAREER-1 (NJ and Canada: 201-848-0310) to order using VISA or MasterCard, or for further information on books from Career Press.

The Career Press, Inc., 3 Tice Road, PO Box 687,
Franklin Lakes, NJ 07417
www.newpagebooks.com
www.careerpress.com

Library of Congress Cataloging-in-Publication Data

Telesco, Patricia, 1960-
    A witch's beverages and brews : magick potions made easy / by
Patricia Telesco.
        p.   cm.
    Includes index.
    ISBN 1-56414-486-0 (pbk.)
    1. Witchcraft. 2. Beverages—Miscellanea. 3. Brewing—Miscellanea.
I. Title.

    BF1572.R4 T447 2000
    133.4'4—dc21   00-033912

This book is dedicated to good friends, without whom there would be little worthy of toasting. Specifically, to Walker, I promise never to serve you anything other than Coors Light and Sam Adams again. Rowan, Kit, and Danya, you can show this to him when he gets uppity.

To Maggie, AJ, Wade, Diane, Betsy, Talyn, Corwyn, Tsa, the Guardians, and many others who never forget a cold beer and a warm smile.

And finally, to all the wonderful festival coordinators everywhere, who deserve far more thanks for their time and efforts than any one dedication can manage. Without you, our community would be sorely wanting. Cheers!

CONTENTS

INTRODUCTION

"Oh, many a peer of England brews,
livelier liquor than the muse;
and malt does more than Milton can,
to justify God's ways to man."

—Alfred E. Houseman

As most people stumble into the kitchen and reach for a morning cup of coffee, they probably do not think of this moment as remotely magickal—except perhaps for that uncanny spiritual pleasure derived from the first sip. Nonetheless, coffee (along with many other beverages) has played an important role in the world's mystical and religious practices! In fact, temple altars from Japan to South America have often been adorned with elaborate cups just waiting to be filled. With what? All manner of drinks including wine, water, beer, milk, or other similar liquids aimed at honoring and appeasing the god or goddess to whom that temple was built.

While this custom seems far removed from our drive-through society, you will still see water- or wine- filled chalices on many church altars today. Even outside this setting there are a lot of beverages that we have come to treasure on a personal, familial, or cultural level. For example, do you prepare eggnog on Yule from an old family recipe or *always* use the same set of glasses to serve out wine for special occasions? These kinds of actions indicate a unique quality in beverages that has captured human imaginations and taste buds for centuries!

This book comes to you with that rich heritage in mind by offering options for an assortment of enchanted brews and beverages that will appease your physical and spiritual thirst. Additionally, you'll find effective ideas for using the folklore and history of various beverages as a way to add culturally or personally significant dimensions to anything you might wish to drink. The liberal mixing of tradition and custom with creativity allows you to draw on the best of the past and present for a potent blend whose energies you internalize when you quaff it!

As you might have gathered by my enthusiasm, I really enjoy the ancient art of brewing as a hobby. But there are plenty of recipes and techniques discussed here for those of you who are time-challenged. The great beauty of beverage magick is that it need not be complex at all. Even the simplest of beverages prepared with willful focus and sound metaphysical methods can have just as potent results as those made diligently from scratch. For example, rather than make a wine or juice yourself, you can simply use the blessing and energizing methods suggested with a store-bought brand. So long as the ingredients in a beverage and your intentions match, there's no limit to the kind of results you can achieve this way.

I offer the recipes and methods in this book as a sensitive exploration of both alcoholic and non-alcoholic beverages as a magickal tool. While many people choose not to imbibe these days, magick recognizes that anything treated respectfully holds the potential for positive energy. Additionally, many alcoholic beverages were considered sacred when served out in a liturgical context. So, even if we decide against consuming alcoholic beverages for personal reasons, that doesn't mean it can't become an offering or libation in the context of a ritual or spell.

Introduction

As with magickal cooking, spiritually enhanced beverages require some thoughtfulness in their making. This book offers you various ways of personalizing recipes so that they reflect your preferred flavors and prevalent needs all in one glass. The appendix of ingredients and magickal correspondences will also help with that process, as will keeping your inventive, intuitive self close by while you work.

By making your own ritual brews, you are partaking in an age-old tradition. No matter the final use of that liquid, this gives you a chance to blend talent, vision, love, and discretion into something tasty and filled to overflowing with blessings. Stir up a witch's brew today!

Part 1

History's
Chalice

CHAPTER 1

THEN AND NOW: RELIGION, MYTH, AND MAGICK

"As he brews, so shall he drink."
—Ben Johnson

"Since nature's holy law is drinking, I'll make the law of nature mine and pledge the universe in wine."
—Tom Moore

The history of beverages and specifically brewing is far more intimately linked with religion, lore, and societal traditions than most people realize. There was even a time when certain beverages had to be prepared by a priest or monk, feeling that the art was a sacred task. Add to that the fact that we still call alcohol "spirits" and continue to toast special occasions with beverages (which is actually a kind of invocation), and you begin to see how much of our drinking customs have a mystical connection—albeit somewhat removed from our modern mind-set, except perhaps in a few spiritual sectors.

Today's witches, for example, are very practical and creative. We look to everything in the world as having potential in our practices, including our foods and beverages. In fact, these hold even more potential because you consume them, literally taking the energy into yourself and accepting it into every cell in your body. Before you can make this huge leap from just grabbing a glass of water to quaffing magick, however, it helps to see from where our methods and ideas on this subject originate.

HISTORICAL AND MAGICKAL ROOTS

To understand the ancient reverence for beverages, we have to turn back the hands of time. In humankind's earlier history, water was not always safe to consume. So when brewing came along it was honored as a gift of the gods that could keep people healthy and make them feel happy. Thus it was that all manner of fermented beverages found their way into healing, the church, social occasions, and magickal methods.

On a far simpler level, the human body requires a certain amount of liquid to survive. So, milk and water held similar places of honor. Milk, for example, often symbolized the Goddess being that it's a beverage produced by woman that literally gives life to a child and protects the baby's health. Water in desert regions was often used as a viable, and very costly, offering to the Divine when needs were pressing. To give of something that was in such short supply surely would get a god or goddess's attention!

Here is a brief overview of the ways in which specific beverages were introduced into religious and magickal settings throughout history:

Beer: Egyptians had beer very early, perhaps as long ago as 6,000 B.C.E. They credited this beverage to the wise god Osiris, and used it in rituals in his honor. They also included beers in their divine myths, and as part of embalming traditions where it (or sometimes wine) was buried with the mummy for that person's enjoyment in the afterlife.

Much later in history we find medieval monks and nuns using beer as part of healing, often adding magickal methods to the preparations neatly disguised with Christian-sounding prayers. In Germany, beer halls were considered one of the few places legal transactions could take place because no one would insult these walls with false intentions. There was even a special profession here for the person who brewed beer for Pagan offerings. That individual was to have no other duties then tending the sacred brews.

In Celtic society, beer was a part of every social occasion and named accordingly. For example, beer for a burial might be called "inheritance beer." In this setting, priests were often in charge of brewing, and it was regarded as quite an honorable vocation.

Coffee: Coffee was (and still is) a well-honored beverage in Arabia, where it is used as part of hospitality rites and in the rituals of the Whirling Dervishes. In this part of the world there is even a patron saint of coffee lovers: Sheikhesh Shadhilly!

Distilled Beverages: These likely originated in Arabic cultures, but this is a best guess by historians, and the early histories of this type of drink are very sketchy. Even so, during the Middle Ages we find people drinking a distilled mixture called Aqua Vitae with dozens of herbs steeped within to insure health and longevity.

Haomas:

A Persian beverage believed to confer longevity to those who consumed it, haomas symbolized the earth's bounty and immortality. It was often used as both an offering for Ormuzd, a greater god, and as a panacea.

Mead:

A type of honey wine very popular among Saxons, it was used as part of wedding rites to insure fertility and love. Many weddings were actually followed by a month (one full moon cycle) of mead drinking which is how we come by the modern phrase "honeymoon." Greeks and Romans alike revered this beverage for its magickal healing qualities, and in ancient Alexandria a cup of mead was often left on tables to invoke the Goddess on the last day of the month.

Milk:

Since the very first mammal suckled its child, there has been milk on this planet. As a symbol of nurturing sustenance and the feminine creative power, there is little else to compare to this beverage. It is not surprising to discover that it was considered a sacred beverage to many mother goddess figures.

As an interesting side note, the domestication of animals in Neolithic times has an extra benefit: ready milk! Rather than gathering it from nuts or having to chase after milk-producing animals, the creatures were at hand, which also meant the milk would not spoil!

Soma: Soma was an herbal beverage created in Central Asia specifically for religious observances. In Hindu tradition it represented faithfulness, friendship, and the spirit of the muse. In fact, the texts of the Rig Veda calls soma "master of a thousand songs" and "leader of sages."

Tea: A very ancient beverage, tea was already a staple trade good in China by 500 C.E. Long before this, however, we discover tea as part of elaborate rituals here, and in other Eastern lands, because it was sacred to Buddha. When tea found its way to Europe and beyond, it quickly became a favorite herb to use in divination.

Tze Mai: This is a mythical immortality beverage in China for which philosophers and priests searched so diligently that they experienced advancements in medicine, science, and geography in the process!

Wine: Numerous sacred texts ranging from the Bible, the Edda, and Ramses IV tablets all speak of wine in a religious setting. In Egypt specifically, wine was considered suited to the gods and goddesses to please their palate, especially Isis. It was also often left with bodies of Pharaohs and other people of import upon mummification. During the reign of Ramses alone, the family donated 250,000 jugs of wine to the temples.

In Greece, people connected wine so strongly with the image of Dionysus that the god himself was said to live in each glass poured out. It's not surprising that we discover a method of divination by wine in this region, and it was also used as part of the traditional rites of passage for young men.

Celts were similarly enamored of wine. Here you could often find families or groups of warriors drinking from one common cup of wine to create unity and kinship among them. Singular cups were also used in wedding rites to link the couple's destiny.

This review is but a short montage from a much larger picture. Beverages have touched nearly every part of human life, from our daily meals to celebrations and the early sciences. At least part of the reason beverages found a comfortable niche in so many settings is because they were included in the great bardic stories told again and again at the fireside and the hearth.

LEGENDS AND LORE

The complete beverage picture includes the great myths and legends woven by storytellers throughout the millennia. Above and beyond the fact that these stories give us a peek into the way ancient people perceived the world and its mysteries, they also reveal a lot of magick and mysticism along the way.

Norse: The Viking people were a hearty lot. Their folklore speaks of an odd custom upon death. Specifically, a person's spirit must consume all the beer spilled during life before entering their final rest in Valhalla. I suspect this story was meant to encourage care with precious beverages, but in looking back over my college years I'm not sure I'd ever reach Valhalla!

Once this vigorous test is passed, the spirit then goes to a special feast that includes mead taken from the base of the Yggdrasil tree, the tree of life. All who partake of this elixir are guaranteed eternal life and well-being in the company of their gods.

Two other great Norse legends (or at least my personal favorites) have to do with Saga and Thor. The first begins with Saga, the patroness of history, being visited by Odin. When he drank of her golden mead-cup, he was given the knowledge of the past, present, and future!

The second story tells us that Loki challenged Thor to a drinking contest. Being the typical trickster, Loki put the end of Thor's drinking horn in the sea. Needless to say, Thor did not win that match, and the ebb tide remains to this day to remind Thor of his attempt at one-upmanship!

German: Speaking of the gods, the stories of Thor indicate he has a special fondness for red beverages. If you offer the first goblet of red wine to him at a wedding, the festivities will be insured of good weather! Another god, Bragi, was in charge of keeping the mead that provided any who drank it with the gift of the muse and poetry. If anyone invoked Bragi's blessing on a cup, they would be granted tremendous orative skills. This connotation slowly transformed to the god's name being used for a modern word: *brag*!

French: The classical story of Tristan and Isolt teaches us much of magickal responsibility. Tristan was a great man, and Isolt a great beauty who was promised to another. Sadly the two drank a love potion, gazed on one another, and were doomed to love from a distance forever. While we do not know what beverages were used for this mixture, we do know one thing: Such powerful brews shouldn't be left laying around!

Chinese: Ancestor worship played a key role in beverage myths and practices here. According to lore, one should always leave fermented beverages for the deceased because it makes a spirit happy (thereby decreasing the chance of being haunted!).

Hindu: An old Indus legend says that the mighty god Indra drank three bowls of soma to absorb its life-giving qualities. Once these were consumed, Indra could then extend his influence throughout the world. Thus, priests and priestesses of Indra often used soma as a preferred beverage to boost magickal power!

Persian: Besides the haomas known for its wealth-producing qualities, another beverage appears in Persian stories called Banga. According to the sage Zoroaster, this drink could produce divine visions. Zoroaster (whose name, by the way, means keeper of old camels) may have been quite correct considering that one ingredient of this mixture was hemp seed!

Egyptian: There are dozens of stories in Egypt that talk about wine and beer, but my favorite begins with Ra. At one point the great god grew weary of

human folly and sent Hathor to destroy everyone. Once his anger quelled, he reconsidered
his own hastiness and tried to get Hathor to stop.
The only way the goddess was going to be ap-
peased was by some fast thinking on Ra's part.
He poured out 7,000 jugs of beer into a field to
where Hathor was heading. When she saw this,
she partook of the beer and her anger disap-
peared. Humankind was saved.

While our world no longer sees brewing as a great mystery
and has lost sight of these wonderful tales in all their charm,
there is no denying the importance of such legends and lore to
our magickal practices. Wiccans remain aware that certain images of the God or Goddess are fond of beverage offerings.
We also know that beverages can be used for asperging, for
libations, for after-ritual enjoyment, and much more if ap-
proached respectfully. At least part of the key to understanding comes from history and heritage. Another key can be found
in the healing arts.

MEDICINAL BEVERAGES

Another reason people held alcoholic beverages in high
esteem can be uncovered in reviewing ancient prescriptions.
Tinctures, beers, wines, and other potent potables were often
used as a base in these blends, neatly covering the taste of a
nasty medicine and getting a stubborn person to rest. Additionally, liqueurs provided a perfect medium into which one could
steep herbs for various remedial results.

How did healers choose the media and blend? Some recipes were carefully guarded and handed down healer to stu-
dent, or through cultural lines. Alternatively, a country healer
might choose his or her blends by their symbolic value, which

is still important to our magick today. For example, red wine was often chosen as a good base into which herbs for blood troubles would be placed. Blood, being red, indicates what color herbs or beverages should be used in the treatment process. This is called the Law of Similars.

Adapting the Law of Similars to any spell or charm is very simple. You look for a beverage whose color matches your goal somehow. So, because red wine was used for blood or heart treatments, how about it as part of a love spell, or one to heal a broken heart?

Here's a list of some of the other beverages used in healing and the symbolic value they have considering their applications:

Cider: This was a chemical also considered a cold drink suited for treating fevers. Adapt this slightly to cool a hot head!

Distilled Beverages: These were used for many different prescriptions, but often in the belief that the more costly the base, the better the results. So, add some expensive liqueur to your spell components to boost power.

Mead: This overall health-promoting beverage could be used to improve mental, spiritual, or physical well-being, or perhaps aid the healthiness of a job situation or relationship. Mead was also a common component in toothache and gum curatives, making a potential addition to communication brews.

Tea: Another fairly widely applied curative, tea probably saw the greatest amount of use with chest congestion and stress-related disorders. This gives it strong connections with the Air element or energy for peacefulness and calming.

Tincture: A tincture blends tea and alcohol into a very mild mixture often applied for spasms of any sort (coughing, twitching, restless fidgeting, etc.). With this in mind, we might use it magickally to calm and pacify erratic energy.

Tonics: By definition, a tonic is any water-based blend used to improve energy, revitalize, stimulate, strengthen, and/or nurture. No tweaking needed here for magickal applications!

Wine: Egyptians used wine in healing because it was associated with the Snake Goddess, who provided health, longevity, and rebirth. Bearing this in mind, it is magickally suited to secure endurance for self or a beloved project, or help with new beginnings.

Another interesting thing about the old remedials is that instructions often include magickal-sounding methods mixed in for good measure. Specific moonsigns were chosen as the best time to create a blend, specific numbers of herbs added into it, and then appropriate chants or prayers said over the finished product.

It should be noted too that many of the beverages that came from the witch's cauldron were effective. For example, the old gag of witches using toads in brewing isn't so crazy sounding when you realize that folkhealers were using toad skin to treat heart problems (toad skin has a chemical similar to digitalis). Likewise, healers in China used bones to treat convulsions even as modern physicians administer calcium!

It was in this manner that the early healers remained aware of their responsibility to the community, and served it with practicality in one hand and magick in the other!

SUMMARY

In our ancestors search to improve their lives, they often looked to beverages as part of the answer, or perhaps part of the question. As they thirsted after understanding and discovered new things, they diligently left us thirst-quenching recipes and lore to ponder. You will find many of those ancient recipes and beliefs in this book so you can partake in the heritage, and hopefully answer part of your own quest in the process. The ultimate goal of a kitchen witch or folk magician is to live the magick, and bringing that special spark to our beverages is one way of doing just that.

FROM CAULDRON TO CUP: MAKING THE MAGICK!

> *"Bread to feed our friendship,*
> *salt to keep it true,*
> *water that's for welcome,*
> *wine to drink for you."*
>
> —W. French

> *"There is naught, no doubt, so much the spirit calms*
> *as rum and true religion."*
>
> —Lord Byron

Bill Moyers in *The Power of Myth* said that "myths are the stories of our search through the ages for truth, for meaning, for significance." To witches, this is a very important statement that we take to heart. As did the cunning folk of old, we look for deeper connotations to global myths and lore and then use that meaning as a motivating force for magickal manifestation!

In Chapter 1, you saw that there are plenty of such stories surrounding beverages. The next logical step becomes looking at how we can apply them effectively in our beverage preparation, serving, and final utilization.

POURING OUT, ASPERGING, ANOINTING, OR BATHING

Before looking at beverages to drink, it should be noted that some liquids were applied in ways of which you might not immediately think. One such custom seen quite frequently is that of pouring out a beverage for magickal effects. Apollonius wrote of the Argonauts pouring mead on the sea before sailing for safe weather.

This custom appears in other cultural settings, too. On New Year's in England, for example, farmers would pour out apple juice or cider onto the groves to insure themselves of a hearty yield the next year. This particular idea is fairly easy for any magickal gardener to use, except perhaps you might want to prepare a liquid that will deter bugs or enrich your soil physically as well as magickally!

A second custom from Europe is that of washing in sacred wells or fonts, or drinking some of the water therein for health. I see no problem with this so long as you know the water is clean. And, because you're a witch, you can even bless your kitchen tap to act in a similar fashion!

The third approach, anointing, isn't quite as common as some of the methods discussed herein. I have, however, seen spells or rituals that call for anointing a person with milk, wine, or steeped herbs in the appropriate location for that ritual. For example, a woman wishing to conceive might be dabbed with milk near her breasts as a kind of sympathetic magick.

A fourth tradition is that of sprinkling out (asperging) a sacred beverage, often to invoke rain, fertility (in people, crops, or cattle), or request protection. To try the rain spell yourself, use water-oriented components in creating the beverage (catnip, daisy, elm, heather, thyme, and tomato are all good examples), dip a broom into it, then shake it on the ground (making the visual appearance of rain). Note that because you are not consuming this liquid, you need not worry about flavor-only symbolic value.

For physical fertility, it's far more productive to prepare a beverage you (or an animal) can consume. This is because the body can better benefit from taking the energy into itself and processing it according to your vision and goal. If you're using it for the fertility of a garden, on the other hand, focus on using soil-enhancing items like those from your compost pile steeped in water.

Finally, in looking at protection we come to a far more familiar custom—baptism. Here water is poured on a child by way of blessing and consecration. Pagans still often perform a similar rite where they introduce a child to the Water element in a naming ceremony. Alternatively, many witches sprinkle water, wine, or other specially prepared beverages around the perimeter of the sacred space to help protect and energize it. Sometimes a bit of this liquid remains on the altar in a cup or cauldron to be shared among the participants. They can take it home after the gathering and dab a little on windows and doors to inspire similar results.

As you can see, this gives you a lot of flexibility in how you use any magickal beverage you create. And I'm not done yet!

LIQUID DIVINATION

Ancient stories are filled with beverages and fortune telling mixed liberally together. Norse legends, for example, say that Bragi's inspiring mead was so potent because it had runes blended within, thereby providing deep insights. More in the realms of documented history, Roman sibyls used wine to encourage altered states of awareness so they could become a Divine oracle. This state was called *enthcos*, which means one with God. Greeks observed any spatters made by wine at gatherings for omens and signs. And in the Middle Ages, the surface of a wine or water cup might be scried for images, by a talented diviner.

Of these methods, I think the scrying or spattering technique is the most serviceable to modern witches. Take a beverage whose color, flavor, or base has symbolic value to the question you have. Pour a little in a dark bowl or cup then follow these instructions based on which method you've chosen:

Scrying

Put a lit candle near the bowl or cup so the flame is reflected in the liquid. Close your eyes for a moment and think of your question. When you have the question fully formulated, open your eyes and watch the surface of the beverage. Don't try to see anything in particular. In fact, let your vision blur a little.

Wait and see what appears. Sometimes you'll see symbols in the light reflections, other times movement or clouds. If the latter, movement up and to the right is a positive response; down and to the left is a negative response. Swirling clouds mean there's no easy answer right now. Symbolic images should be interpreted according to the picture (you may find a dream dictionary helps with this).

If the reading is particularly positive you may wish to drink the beverage afterwards to internalize that future. However, a negative reading might be better poured out to release those bad "vibes" so the earth can carry the energy away from you.

Spattering

Pour your beverage of choice into a bowl and have a white, absorbent piece of paper nearby. Stir the liquid clockwise with your strong hand while you think of your question. Next, either pour a couple of drops of this liquid onto the paper, or sprinkle some out with your finger tips (flicking it lightly off so you don't stain your clothing or a table cloth).

From here you can proceed in one of two ways. Some people just let the pattern dry and look for meaning in it then. Other people like to fold the paper while thinking of their question, then open it and observe the results, somwhat like finding images in an ink blot! Both approaches work perfectly well. Just choose one that suits you and feels right at the moment.

In terms of interpreting the resulting patterns, books on tea leaf reading often prove quite helpful here. The images tend to have similar "rough" qualities. You can use the center of the paper to represent the present (or very intimate matters) and the outer edges to represent the future and cursory matters. Where a pattern lands will then help you understand its meaning more thoroughly.

POTENT POTIONS

The most popular way to use beverages for magick by far is that of potion making. It's difficult to read any old metaphysical treatise without stumbling over witch's brews scattered throughout the pages. These recipes include nearly every fathomable ingredient for an equally impressive number of applications. Here's just a sampling of some of the old potions I came across in my readings:

→ Jet powdered in water to keep snakes at bay, or steeped in wine to cure elf magick. Note the second blend must be consumed over nine days to break the spell (Anglo-Saxon charm).

→ Angelica in vinegar to banish negative magick (yuck, I suspect it turns stomachs, too). This comes from France.

→ Vervain gathered by a new moon and drunk in juice before sunrise for devotion (European tradition).

- → Boneset tea to repel evil spirits (Saxon charm).

- → Carrot and sunflower seeds consumed in wine to promote fertility (England).

- → Chrysolite powdered in wine to negate foolish thoughts (Greece).

- → Elder and borage picked on Midsummer Day and drunk twice a month with water to insure youth (England).

- → Pine resin mixed with water and wine to encourage longevity (China).

- → Saffron tincture for offsetting the effects of jaundice (Asia).

- → Dill wine to cure hiccups (Mediterranean region).

- → Egg and whiskey blended together to cure dysentery (Ireland).

- → Ambergris in coffee to encourage passion (Europe).

- → Bindweed potion to deter pain (Germany).

These potions often included subtle symbolic values that you might not notice immediately. For example, the use of saffron against jaundice is significant because this herb is ruled by the sun—a type of light that still helps this condition. Likewise, bindweed is chosen for pain because of its "binding" name, and elder and borage were picked on Midsummer Day because that's when magickal herbs are thought to be most potent!

Most often the symbolism in these potions could be identified by a color, number, or timing. You may want to use some of these ideas in preparing your own witchy beverages and brews, so please refer to Appendix B.

MAGICKAL CONCOCTING

Beyond the symbolic value you give to your brews, there are other simple things to consider for magickal preparations. First, make sure you're in the right frame of mind for a spiritual undertaking. If you're tired, sick, angry, or feeling "off," that negative energy can easily spill into your preparation, so it might be best to wait unless the need is pressing.

Also think about the environment in which you're working. It's prudent to have a clean, physically and psychically clear work space. Remove items that distract you from anything other than the task at hand.

Next, make sure you have all the ingredients and tools you need. It's very distracting to stop a spell or incantation in the middle because you forgot something. Such distractions can cause the energy to go awry.

If you wish you can play music, light candles, burn incense, chant, pray, or even create a sacred space within which to prepare the brew. The first three are pretty easy to figure out—find music that uplifts your spirit, candles of a thematic color, and incense whose aroma matches your goal. Chanting and/or prayer can be rhymed, take the form of an incantation, or whatever suits your mood.

If you're unfamiliar with making sacred space, this really is a matter of changing your attitude. Approach your work area like you might a church. Then ask your vision of the sacred, and the four powers of Earth, Air, Fire, and Water to watch over your efforts and you won't go far wrong. It is best that you find a way to do this that's comfortable, otherwise you'll be so self-conscious that it will be hard to focus on the magick you're creating.

Remember to keep your purpose foremost in your mind while you prepare the beverage. If it's something you're going to age and/or store away, make sure to label it creatively (include ingredients, timing, etc., if you think it important) so you know for what it's intended. For example, a love beverage might be called Raspberry Romance if it was based in raspberries. This also eliminates the chance that a friend with raspberry allergies might sip your brew! Likewise, if you've made a brew specifically for asperging or libations, make sure you label it as NOT FOR CONSUMPTION to avoid mishaps.

The great beauty of beverage magick is that it requires few tools and very little time to make something potent, meaningful, and tasty.

DRINKING VESSELS

One really simple way of adding meaning to your beverage is by using special serving vessels whose color, shape, or imagery accents your goal in some way. Our ancestors used everything from bowls and drinking gourds to elaborate horns and gem-encrusted chalices for their beverages. For example, rulers often drank from an amethyst cup to safeguard themselves from drunkenness. The stone itself was said to have this property, but more likely the idea was to make it appear as if they were having wine instead of water! Another example comes from Norse legend, where stories tell of runes being carved into cups to protect the bearer from being poisoned. Should anything ill touch that cup, the runes would cause it to shatter or the beverage within to turn a hideous color, thereby marking the treachery.

In Gypsy and Celtic tradition, couples being handfasted or married would drink from one cup to link their destiny. In Germany, pledge or oath cups appeared during contractual agreements. In this case a sip sealed the deal! In all three of these settings refusing a cup from one's host was a tremendous insult, whereas accepting it also graciously accepted the hospitality extended.

Nothing says we can't follow these example with magickally significant adaptations! Bowls, for example, might be best suited to beverages we make for our pets. A lovely red goblet, on the other hand, might be used for a love potion. Bear in mind that overall, cups represent the Goddess because of the womb-like shape. If you want something more strongly aligned with the God aspect, look for squared-off drinking vessels.

Similarly we can consider how many cups should be used to hold our finished brews. One cup is fantastic to symbolize unity and harmony, while two might be better suited to a mutual partnership. In a group setting, each person could dip his or her cup into a communal cauldron—here the cauldron becomes the emblem of fellowship, while the singular cup represents the importance of each individual to that group. Really, the options here are as endless as your imagination will allow.

TOASTS

We talked briefly in Chapter 1 about toasts being a kind of prayer or invocation. This tradition is very old. In the Zend Avesta (sacred Persian texts) there are many illustrations of a celebrant or priest raising a cup to the sky saying "I claim thee, O yellow one, for inspiration, for strength, for vigor." The "yellow one" is h•Haomas, but the rest of the toast is certainly a welcoming of Spirit, or more specifically the energy of the beverage.

Exactly what form a toast takes depends on the purpose of the beverage or the theme of a gathering. For example, if your group was doing a love ritual honoring Aphrodite, it might be good to use a quote from Madge Merton who said "Great spirit of the grape—delirious kiss of lips immortal from the sky, rare nectar of Olympus born of bliss, bright spark of Aphrodite's eye!" Believe it or not, I found that in a book dedicated to toasting!

Now, if you're someone who doesn't have quote books handy for just such occasions, fret not! There's no reason you can't make up your own magickal toasts. They need not rhyme or have fancy words. They do, however, need to be heartfelt and meaningful to you. Words have great power to help your magick along, especially words spoken with conviction and focus.

FOCUSED DRINKING

Speaking of focus, it is very important to keep your attention directed to your goal as you enjoy magickal beverages too. Remember that every drop carries with it a spark of energy that mingles with your aura and every cell in your body. When created and consumed correctly, this can change the entire pattern of the energy that you carry, both within and without. Such transformations lie at the very heart and soul of what magick is all about, so drink thoughtfully and expectantly!

BEVERAGES TO ENHANCE FOOD

Because when we drink we often eat too, why not combine the two activities into something magickally oriented? You could, for example, add an energized beverage into a soup, stew, or casserole. One illustrative idea along this line is putting a little plum wine into your chicken stew for abundance or romance. Or, marinate and baste the main dish with the significant beverage (like mead over ham for happiness and health). Here are some other ideas for you to try:

→ Start a glaze base with a beverage, adding butter, sugar, and/or herbs as desired for more meaning and flavor.

→ Use beverages as part of desserts (or dessert toppings). One example here would be making a syrup out of rose wine and pouring it over angel food cake for sweet, innocent love.

→ Add the beverage to sauce and gravy. You don't need a lot. The energy pattern created by your magick will disperse itself into the whole blend even when you use only a drop or two!

→ Consider beverages as flavorful components in jellies, jams, and conserves (be sure to adjust any other liquid proportions accordingly). There's some nice symbolism here of having the magick "jell" or "solidify."

I cannot stress enough just how much variety and flexibility you have available to you in beverage magick. Try not to get stuck in a rut as you go along. While it's good to develop skill in one area and build on that, it's also good to play a little and let your imagination run wild. Joy has a lot of magick in it without any trappings—so brew and enjoy yourself. In the words of Homer:

> *And wine can, of their wits beguile*
> *make the sage frolic and the serious smile!*

HELPFUL HINTS

This chapter will provide you with insights about brewing alcoholic beverages and other rather unique items such as pop that many people have probably never tried making. If you find you have trouble getting the recipes in the book to work right, this section will help you over the natural stumbling blocks that come with the learning process.

Also, if you find you don't have the time to make these items from scratch, don't despair. There is nothing that says you can't thoughtfully buy a prepared item, bless it, add some flavorings, and stir up the magick with just as much success!

Eight years ago, with the help of my husband, I haphazardly worked through the very first batch of home brew our family ever enjoyed. All things considered, that experiment was very successful and also very contagious. We kept finding new combinations of fruits, juices, and spices to try. Slowly this process refined itself into a few favored recipes, at least one of which is trusted to only a handful of close friends.

The ideas and advice offered in this section come from my own simplified experiences. If you are already an accomplished brewer, you may find some of the techniques presented here (and the rest of the book) a little rudimentary. Mostly, they have been assembled for folks who do not have access to fancier brewing equipment and supplies, or those who prefer using less specialized methods.

There is no reason not to employ these formulas using better accoutrements and tactics should you desire. Most of the systems portrayed generate brews that closely resemble historical wines, beers, etc. More refined procedures and tools produce beverages closer to modern standards, taste, and familiarity.

BASIC BREWING TOOLS

→ Gallon-sized screw top or cork bottles.

→ Balloons and rubber bands, which make excellent makeshift fermentation locks.

→ Strainers, cheesecloth, or gauze to filter out sediments. I have found that bits of nylon, sheer silk, and other thin, clean scraps of material function as makeshift strainers.

→ Mixing bowls, preferably stoneware or pottery.

→ Freezer-friendly pans (for frappes).

→ Large cooking pans that are not aluminum.

→ Funnels in various sizes.

→ Large wooden spoon or other stirring utensil and a slotted spoon to remove large brewing components (fruit, etc.).

→ Sharp knife or athame for cutting herbs and fruits.

→ Mortar and pestle to macerate root herbs such as ginger.

→ Active bread, wine, or beer yeast.

→ Accurate measuring tools.

→ A clean, tight woven, cotton cloth to cover beverages during the first fermentation. Clean dish towels work.

→ A cool, dark storage area.

→ A must jar. This is a type of plastic or glass container where brewing leftovers (fruit, spices, bits of wine) go. Some people use must for making jams, jellies, sauces, and the like.

Non-Essential Tools (But Fun Ones)

→ A hydrometer. This measures the alcohol content of your finished wines, meads, etc.

→ Fermentation locks. These come in various sizes to keep your bottles from accidentally exploding when pressure builds. They are inexpensive (usually under $1 each) and keep you from having to clean up a very sticky mess.

Pressure in brewing bottles becomes quite volatile in the initial stages of fermentation. This can cause bottles to explode, throwing glass shards everywhere. Therefore, commit yourself to either monitoring your brews on a daily basis (burping the bottles), to using balloons on the bottle tops during early fermentation, or to buying some fermentation locks. After having cleaned up more than one explosion in my cellar, trust me when I say this is important.

→ Camden tablets. These help the pace of fermentation to be steady. Also sometimes called "nutrients."

→ Fermentation casks—beautiful wooden casks that make your cellar look like the brewing closets of olde. These also give a distinctive flavor to wines and beers often peculiar to the type of wood the barrel is made from. An alternative is a glass carboy (price about $15) with cap and stopper.

→ Clarifying tools. These usually consist of a glass jar and special tubing that allows only the clear wine to be siphoned off your fermenting container.

+ Corn sugar—makes beverages ferment more quickly and have clearer flavors.

+ Sparkaloid—helps to clarify beers.

+ Sterilizer or antioxidant (450 milligrams sodium metabisulphite per gallon). Be aware that some people have negative reactions to sulphites.

+ Citric acid—may be used in place of citrus fruit when you want the content but not the flavor.

+ Sorbistat—prevents refermentation once a beverage has been boiled to stop the process.

BEER

"Beer is liquid Bread."

—Liebig

Known to the Anglo-Saxons as breowan, Germans as briuwan, Norse as brugga, French as brasser, and Irish as brach, by any name beer is beverage of "everyman." This symbolism seems to remain with us magickally where beer can represent friendly gatherings, mutual interests, friendship, relaxation, and similar themes. There are certainly other applications for beer, but considering the way beer continues to be used in our society, these symbols seem the most congruent.

In Strabo XVII 2.5 we read, "Beer is in use with a number of peoples, and each one brews it somewhat differently." It is because of this variety that giving a basic beer recipe is difficult, at best. Every cultural group and nearly every brewer approaches it differently. So, instead of a static process here, I'd like to provide you with helpful hints when you find you're having trouble with the beer recipes.

Helpful Hints for Beer Making

+ If possible, always use dry beer yeast versus a bread yeast. Beer yeast is always labeled for top (ale) or bottom (lager) fermentation and yields a much clearer beverage with no lingering "yeasty" flavor. Generally, home brewers are more successful with ale yeast, which works well at room temperature.

    Please note that the brewers yeast frequently sold in health food stores *cannot* be used for actual brewing. It is inert and will not encourage proper fermentation.

+ Of hops readily available through brewing stores, Cluster, Cascade, Hallertau, and Saaz are some of the best.

+ Irish moss, if added to the boiling process for the last few minutes, helps clarify your beer.

+ Whenever possible, use spring water as a base for your beer. This is especially important for people who live in cities with poorer quality water. Any sediments in the tap water can drastically change the flavor of your finished product.

+ When you notice that the bottom of your fermenting jars look as if they are covered with film, it is time to rack off the clear liquid. Leaving sediment in the bottom of the jar makes for bitter beers. Racking may be done either by carefully pouring off the top portion of the beer and rinsing the bottle or by siphoning.

BEER – NON-ALCOHOLIC

In actuality, these are "small" beers in that a minute amount of alcohol content is created in the production. If you feel you need to totally eliminate this, once the beverage is ready to drink, boil it (no hotter than 180 degrees), effectively evaporating any alcohol, then chill and serve. The only problem with boiling is that it deters the "head" of the beer. To compensate, prepare your batches slightly stronger than desired, boil them at 180 degrees for 15 minutes, then serve with a little seltzer water to achieve "fizz."

These beverages should not be stored for more than four to six weeks if you want to keep the alcohol content at a minimum. To alleviate this problem, after the first brief fermentation period keep the bottles in a refrigerator. This will inhibit the yeast, while extending the shelf life to about four months.

FRAPPES

Frappes are semi-frozen drinks served in iced cups. Usually frappes are made from fruit juices or flavored waters and sweetener, which are blended then half frozen to take on a snow-like consistency. To quote modern commercials, in this beverage "the thrill is the chill!"

In all recipes provided in this book, except where noted, the following basic directions should be used. As is the case with soda pop, it is best to use a sweetener in syrup form to mix evenly with the juice(s). Next, you combine the syrup with hot juice and flavor with any additional ingredients desired. Please add these components slowly, taste testing for personal preference at this point. Cool and pour into a shallow pan for freezing. Stir this occasionally so the liquid freezes evenly.

When the entire batch has equal amounts of ice throughout, remove it from the pan and crush it with the flat of a wooden spoon. Once a uniform consistency is reached, fluff with a fork in the same manner you would beat an egg. The beverage can be placed in a tall, chilled glass at this point and garnished with fruit, flavored whipped cream, some sundae syrup, or whatever seems fitting.

The magickal symbolism here varies according to your perspective. You can freeze energy with frappes as you initially freeze the beverage, break up a type of energy when you beat it, or lift energy by fluffing the iced pieces.

JUICING

"Tis a little thing to give a cup of water yet its draught of cool refreshment drained by fevered lips may give a shock of pleasure to the frame more exquisite than when nectarean juice penetrates the life of joy in happiest hours"
—Sir Thomas N. Talfourd

Most of us live in a state of perpetual busyness. Any number of daily duties can leave little time for three square meals a day. This makes easy, healthful beverages very important to just maintaining health, let alone spiritual wellness. That is probably why juicing became a popular "fad" of the 1990s.

Most fruits and vegetables contain considerable levels of fiber, iron, calcium, potassium, vitamins B and C, beta carotene, and sodium, all of which can be beneficial to most diets. Some of these beverages help stave off cravings for candy by supplying our bodies with natural sugars. Thus, juicing can be an integral part of sound weight loss efforts, with no artificial colors or flavors to hinder revitalization.

You do not *have* to buy a special juicer for this product. A good blender or food processor and straining equipment will do. The major advantage to juicers is that they are specifically constructed to make your job a lot easier. If you decide to purchase one, look for good quality, safety, and a clearly stated warrantee.

In general, juiced products represent health and healing; however, because you blend them, other types of energy can certainly be whipped in for good measure! Also, health can relate to many things: the healthy nature of a situation, the health of a relationship, the health of your garden, and so forth. So, get creative!

General Juicing Instructions

First, make sure to clean your ingredients under warm water. If possible, buy organically grown fruits and vegetables to eliminate the ingestion of pesticides. Remove all leaves, seeds, rinds, and bruised parts before putting the components in your blender/juicer. With the exception of potatoes, fruits and vegetables are predominantly juiced raw to obtain the highest content of nutrients. Then all that remains is pulping the ingredients thoroughly with your equipment.

If you do not want chunky drinks, use a good sieve and strain off the juice. To recycle the left over pulp, put it in an equal portion of hot water and bring to a low rolling boil for one hour and strain again. This juice will not be as high in vitamins as the first extraction, but it will use your components economically. Be sure to refrigerate any unused portions. The remaining pith can be composted.

An alternative means of recycling pulp is to make fruit and vegetable wines out of it. In this case, you will be substituting an equal amount of pulp for whatever fruit or vegetable your recipe calls for. Note: you may find you wish to add a little extra pulp since some of the flavor has already been used up.

The remaining pulp, if any, can be composted.

MEAD

"From the mead horn—the pure and shining liquor, which the bees provide but do not enjoy, Mead distilled I praise."
—*Book of Taliesin,* Mabinogion

There are several types of mead. Melomel is mead that has fruit or fruit juice in it. Pymet is mead made with grape juice. Metheglin is made with herbs and hippocras is made with both grape juice and spices. The greatest amount of success in mead making comes through a little experimentation with your components, and contentious skimming of honey sediment, which rises to the top of your pot during boiling. Also, when possible, try to purchase a good quality, raw honey and mead yeast or sparkling wine yeast. These improve the overall body and taste of the finished mead.

Basic Mead Recipe
(See Appendix D for U.S. to metric conversions.)

This recipe will serve as a good foundation for all your efforts in mead-related drinks. Simply change fruits, fruit juices, and spices for different and uniquely flavored results.

All proportions given are for one gallon yields.

1 gallon water   3 pounds dark honey
2 oranges   1 lemon
1/2 package sparkling yeast

Directions: Place the honey with water in a two-gallon pot over a medium flame. To this, slice in the oranges and lemon in large enough pieces to easily remove by slotted spoon later. Bring the mead to a gentle rolling boil, skimming off any scum which rises to the top over the next hour. Strain out the fruit pieces and any spices you may have added, and let this cool to lukewarm. Meanwhile, suspend the yeast (dissolve it) in 1/4 cup warm water. Stir this into the liquid only after the mead reaches room temperature or you'll kill the yeast. Allow this mixture to sit with a woven cover (like a dish towel) for seven days until the first fermentation has slowed considerably. Strain again, trying to pour off only the clearer top fluids into a bottle to age. These bottles should be lightly corked for about two months, or fixed with a fermentation lock. Strain again, then tightly seal them for six months before using.

MEAD – NON-ALCOHOLIC

"In a large silver urn, pour six cups of kindness, five cups of tenderness, four cups of affection, three cups of understanding, two cups of good nature, one whole cup of truth, one half cup of smiles, one teaspoon of tears...stir well."

—Count De Mauduit

I made an interesting discovery when I first tried to find recipes for non-alcoholic mead. Right through the 1920s, mead was not considered a spirituous beverage! This is probably due to the fact that mead was made very thick, with more than the necessary amount of honey, fermented only a short time, then drawn off and mixed with juice or carbonated water (circa 1919).

The ratio given in a turn-of-the-century cookbook for the second option was 2 oz. mead (aged about three weeks) to 12 oz. additive. The original preparation was anywhere from 1/5 to 1/2 honey by proportion to the water base. This would yield a beverage with a root-beer-like head and only the very slightest percentage of alcohol.

In the interest of pleasing the purist, I have provided recipes for straight, fruited, or spiced meads without using yeast. This eliminates the need to wait for the beverage to age. Just be careful taste-testing during preparation. Because there is no yeast to eat up your honey, if you make it too sweet, that's the way it will stay unless diluted or infused with juice.

Additionally, because there is no alcohol to act as a preservative, I do not suggest making any more mead than you will consume in a three-week period. Honey, fruits, and flowers have the capacity to carry wild yeast that can slowly activate and begin fermenting. The other half of this picture is mead gone bad, mold and all. Keep your finished meads in a cool storage space in airtight containers for best results.

Basic Recipe

1 gallon water	1/2 to 1 pound of honey
1 lemon, juiced	1 orange, juiced

Directions: Bring your water to a low, rolling boil in a pan that is not aluminum. Stainless steel or stoneware is recommended. Slowly add the honey, allowing it to fully mingle with the water. Taste periodically until a personally pleasant level of sweetness and honey flavor is achieved. Add juices of the fruit at this point and bring the entire mixture to a full boil. Scum from the honey will start to rise. It is very important that you skim this off until it all but disappears from the top of the pot. Doing this will help your mead to be clearer and less heavy in body. Finally, cool the mixture completely and place in sterilized bottles with secure tops for storage.

Please note that your mead can be served hot with a cinnamon stick, or cold over crushed ice with a slice of lemon or orange to refresh the flavor.

SODA POP

"Let us have wine and women, mirth and laughter,
sermons and soda-water the day after."

—Lord Byron

A century ago, malted milk shakes and soda pop were dispensed carefully by the glassful, often by the local pharmacist, as the latter was sometimes prescribed for health. Also known as sweet water and fizz water, soda pop is one of the largest beverage industries in the United States.

To get an idea about the beginnings of fou
let's look to one company. Its originator, Cha
dream to establish mail-order sales of hon
kits. Mr. Hires carefully selected 18 ingredie
and herbs, and packaged them with direc

housewife. This package sold for 25 cents and made five gallons of root beer. Slowly, the Hires Root Beer company formed, and with them a number of other popular favorites followed.

People today continue to enjoy soda pop, malteds, and other "fountain" drinks. As of 1982, each person in the United States consumed approximately 38 gallons of pop per year. In other words, we annually drink as many soft drinks (and related beverages) as we do water.

From a magickal perspective, I see soda pop as youthful, invigorating, uplifting, and happy like its bubbles.

Soda Pop Basics

Older formulas for soda pop call for forced carbonation or the addition of yeast. Yeast leaves an average alcohol content of about 1 percent, which is not acceptable if one is allergic to alcohol! Thankfully, home-brewed soda pop today can be much simpler. The basic formula is carbonated water, sweetener, and added flavoring(s). Sweeteners may be adjusted to suit your dietary needs, including substituting honey or Nutrasweet for sugar.

Make a syrup of your sweetening agent so it mixes well with room temperature soda water. The proportions are the same for honey and sugar; two cups sweetener to one cup water, brought to a low rolling boil then refrigerated. Then, you can make soda pop by the glass using 1 1/2 cups carbonated water and 1 to 2 tsp. syrup plus your fruit, vegetable, or flower essences and extracts. Choose flavorings made by juicing (see the previous section), or those readily available in the supermarket's cooking aisle.

If you don't like the taste of plain soda water, try ginger ale instead. This makes a zestier drink. Additionally, please take care to add your sweetener slowly. Sugars activate the carbonation even further to the point where your glass may over.

WINE

"Here with a loaf of bread, beneath the bough,
a flask of wine, a book of verse
and thou beside me singing in the wilderness"

—Omar Khayyam

Wine in general is considered the beverage of the gods. It is a type of ambrosia, being used in magick and in religion for everything from offerings and libations to oath taking and oracles. Thus, of all the brewing projects in this book, wine is my favorite to make when time allows. It is a simple pleasure, but a divine one.

As with meads, the procedure for wine is fairly simple. First and foremost, use quality ingredients. Once you refine your talents, it stands to reason that better quality components yield more pleasant wines. At first, using less costly constituents is sensible. Once you get past that point, allow your budget to stretch a bit and you won't be disappointed by the results.

Secondly, take extra care when straining wines. The more sediments you eliminate, the easier it becomes to clarify your beverages. When trying to separate clearer wine from its sediment after the first fermentation, either siphon it off or pour very carefully so the fruit and dead yeast does not enter the new container. This is also a good time to check flavor and add more sugar for sweeter wines.

One of the reasons I love making tea wines is the fact that they rarely need a lot of siphoning (to my thinking—the less fuss the better). By cleverly buying fruity or spicy tea bags, and mixing and matching them, you can come up with wines that have a very full flavor and no sediment to strain out! There are some good examples of tea wines sprinkled throughout this book.

Next is care with corking. If you tighten your tops or corks too soon and leave the bottles unattended, they will explode from early fermentation pressure buildup. That is why I recommended the use of a balloon secured with a rubber band, fermentation locks, or daily "burping" at the outset of this chapter. Because you cannot always control the temperature at which your wines will be fermenting, don't forget this step or you may have a mess on your hands.

The final process is called racking, which is somewhat connected to straining. After the second fermentation, the wine rests in its final container. Lay these so they tilt slightly downward, keeping the corks damp. Initially every month a certain amount of sediment will appear in the bottle. Pour off the clear wine, rinse the containers and rebottle on a regular basis.

As you rack, keep one spare bottle of each batch of wine to refill any air spaces left after siphoning and rebottling. As you follow this procedure, the need to rack the wine decreases and your wine will clarify to look closer to store-bought blends.

Basic Wine

Because the procedure for wine making is pretty standard, instead of including a lot of repetitious directions in this book, this recipe will serve as a foundation for all those that follow. Any variations on this, distinct to a particular recipe, will be noted. All proportions are for one-gallon yields. Recipes may be halved or doubled.

1-2 pounds fruit	spices to taste
1 12 oz. can frozen juice	2-3 pounds sugar
1 gallon water	slice of lemon or orange
1 tea bag	1/3 pkg. wine yeast

Directions: If using spices, place these first in your water and simmer for 30 minutes until a tea-like substance is formed. For spicier drinks, leave the herbs in the water while you add fruit, juice, tea bags, lemon/orange, and sugar. Bring everything to a low rolling boil for 15 minutes, then reduce heat for another 15 minutes. Cool to lukewarm. Meanwhile in a small separate container dissolve the wine yeast in 1/4 cup warm (not hot) water. Let this sit for a minimum of 20 minutes to work before stirring it into the cooled juices.

Leave the entire blend in your pan (preferably not aluminum) over night with a heavy cloth or dish towel over top. In the morning, strain the fruit (and herbs if they were left in) out of the juices and let sit covered in a warm area for another 24 hours. Strain again and move to a loosely covered glass container for one month. As fermentation slows, activity in the container will decrease (less bubbles) and you can move the beverage into smaller bottles for racking. Strain or siphon the wine into your chosen containers to further clarify it, corking loosely for another two to three weeks. If the corks pop out frequently, you know it is too soon for final capping.

All wines should be stored in a dark cool place. Depending on how dry you like your beverages, eight months to three years aging time produces tasty wines. You will have to experiment to find exactly when you are content with the flavor. At this point, in order to stop fermentation, you may either refrigerate your wine, or bring it to a low rolling boil, then bottle again in air tight containers. I usually age wine for about eight months, which yields a sweeter, but not too heavy-bodied beverage.

Hint: At first, match your ingredients by flavor such as apples, apple juice, and apple tea. Apples and grapes are two excellent fruits to start with, almost always yielding positive results. Later, once you feel more certain of the procedure, try mixing and matching your fruits and juices.

WINE – FLOWER AND VEGETABLE

China and Japan were probably the first lands to discover the wonders of brewing with flowers. This was partially due to the obsession Asian peoples had with cooking as an art. What better to grace any lovely dish or sweet cup than the crowning glory of the natural world: flowers.

In China, flower petals scented some of the most exquisite and highly desired teas. In Japan, the chrysanthemum was the flower of choice, with a special celebration in its honor. On the 9th day of the 9th moon (early September), a wine steeped with chrysanthemum petals was given to the emperor to insure long life and encourage poetic muse. In feudal times, the Shogun met with all his samurai on this day. Presently, the tradition continues with competitive flower shows.

Later, during the Middle Ages, petaled beverages (and foods) found their way to Europe with a flurry. Flower and vegetable wines and liquors established a place on the table alongside the more traditional fruit preparations. They were so admired as to become a welcome addition to royal gatherings.

In preparing your own fruit and vegetable wines, two factors rise above all others as crucial for success. The first is freshness. Flowers can be bought dried, but are more effective when freshly harvested. When gathering petals (only petals—no green parts) do so just after the dew evaporates, no later than 10:30 a.m. This helps the petal retain its essential oil. Handle them carefully, storing in a muslin or nylon mesh bag, and use them as soon as possible. Once wilted, their taste is far less enjoyable.

For vegetables, again dried components can be substituted. Even so, nothing beats freshly grown for fullness of flavor. Fresh vegetables have the additional benefit of much higher vitamin contents. Their juices may be easily extracted into the brewing pot.

The second consideration is temperature. Flowers are especially sensitive to heat. When starting a batch of brew with flower petals, you will not be boiling as with many other preparations. Instead, use lower temperatures until petals turn translucent to extract the oils, then strain the liquid to prepare it for the rest of the process. Slower cooking with vegetables yields more pleasant results as well.

WINE ~ NON-ALCOHOLIC

Wines, like beer, cannot be properly prepared at home without some amount of fermentation. Because wine, by definition, is fermented fruit juice, somehow the effect in taste just wouldn't be the same. Because of this, I have employed a similar method in preparing wines as those which are used for homemade soda pop. As with the beers, you can eliminate any alcohol content by boiling, then rejuvenate the bubbles with carbonated water. Additionally, one part soda to one part soft wine makes an effective non-alcoholic wine cooler where the bubbles help carry your magick to the surface!

Basic Recipe (for six 12 oz. bottles)

1 Tbsp. extract or flavoring
72 oz. juice

3/4 cups sugar
1/16 tsp. yeast

Basic Directions: Heat your juice(s) in a large kettle until it is lukewarm. Dissolve the sugar, feeling free to add more if you want a sweeter wine. Likewise, dissolve the yeast and add any flavorings desired during this process. It is a good idea to test the beverage at this point for full-bodied flavor, adding more extract if needed.

Next, move the wine into clean glass bottles that can be either capped (like pop), corked, or sealed with a secure screw top. Keep the bottles in a warm (not hot) area for about four days. Open one carefully to see if it is bubbly enough for your tastes. If not, allow to sit about two days more. Store these in the refrigerator to inhibit further fermentation (and possible explosion of the bottles due to pressure).

Part 2

The Recipes

*"The thirsty earth soaks up the rain
and drinks, and gapes for drink again
and plants suck in the earth and air
with constant drinking lush and fair.
Fill all the glasses then, for why
should every creature drink, but I?"*

—Abraham Cowley

INTRODUCTION

"When the wine goes in, strange things come out."
—Johann Christoph Friedrich Von Schiller

Now comes the fun part—getting your hands into the proverbial cauldron! Even though you're going to be working magick into your brews, that doesn't mean your rational mind has to go by the wayside. For example, don't follow a recipe whose ingredients you don't like. Potions meant for consumption won't do much good if you're more focused on the yucky taste than on the energy in the beverage!

Speaking of which, some people might feel a little squeamish about the recipes that use flowers herein. This is the one time when I will suggest you experiment a little. I was amazed at the wonderful teas and wines roses produce, and these have now become among my favorite brewing ingredients. You might find yourself pleasantly surprised by this, or many other petals, too!

Another good precaution is a simple one: Don't make anything to which you might have an allergic reaction, and don't share homemade beverages with others without telling them the ingredients if you think allergies might be a problem. After all, we want our magick to have only the best possible effects. Besides, there's nothing that says you can't adjust recipes so long as the meaningfulness remains intact. In fact, tinkering with recipes seems to be a time-honored tradition among cooks that kitchen witches joyfully continue.

MUNDANE CONSIDERATIONS

My personal belief is that practicality consists of common sense, mingled with frugality, humor, creative insight, and a little fortitude for good measure. Thus, this section about rather mundane considerations acts as a foundation to any type of beverage-making effort. While some instructions are going to be unique to specific recipes, these sensible suggestions are universal.

First, collect glass bottles in various shapes, sizes, and colors into which you can put your magickal beverages. Make sure to sterilize them for safety reasons. Also collect corks or suitable airtight tops for those bottles. If you're planning to make homemade wine or beer, you also want to have some balloons that act as temporary corks. The balloons stay in place until fermentation decreases enough to put a secure top on the bottle without it constantly popping off.

When you first start making beverages, I usually suggest getting really good at one category of brew first, then going on to others. Pick a category that you like and become an expert. Everything you learn in the process will make other brewing efforts much easier and more successful. Specifically, you'll begin to know nature's chemistry—the idiosyncrasies in various fruits and spices that can make or break the results of your efforts. For example, knowing that strawberries ferment very quickly will help you avoid messy, sticky bottle explosions.

Additionally, your first beverage efforts should be done with simple, cost-effective ingredients. This way if you don't get it right, you haven't spent a fortune. And don't be overly critical with yourself if you have a flop or two. It's quite common, especially in mead, wine, and beer brewing. Practice does make perfect, and you always learn something new from the failures. For example, a friend of mine couldn't figure out why his wine recipe didn't ferment. I found out that he had altered the recipe and decreased the sugar. Consequently, the yeast didn't have enough to eat and the wine never "took." We were actually able to remedy this by warming the whole mixture, adding more sugar, and then bringing in some fresh yeast.

The lesson here is simple: Be careful how you tweak your recipes. If you don't like using teas, for example, some spices like gingerroot can provide tannin, which is necessary to brewing certain kinds of wines and meads. Cross-referencing sources can prove very helpful too—after all, as a brewer I write about things I enjoy drinking, not necessarily everything that *you* will like! In your search for books, watch local secondhand shops that often carry old collections of recipes for very reasonable prices.

Another important thing to do for yourself is date your beverages. Some wines and meads safely age for years, while other drinks are designed for almost immediate use. Dating your bottles will help you avoid getting a mouthful of vinegar, or something equally unpleasant. And while you're labeling, put on the ingredients, the magickal methods (if you wish), and so on. This way you have all the information you need in one spot.

Finally, as you're using or adapting these recipes, please bear in mind that not all herbs used in magick are safe for consumption. If a recipe has an ingredient you have not tried before, or if you're thinking of adding an herb but don't know if it's edible, don't use it! Let common sense prevail.

USING THIS BOOK

Some people reading this book may have never tried to make their own wines, teas, beers, or soda pop. In the interest of not repeating basic recipes, there will be a reference to the step-by-step instructions to making more difficult blends, which were detailed in Chapter 3. As you come across preparations that you're unfamiliar with, go to Chapter 3 and read over the instructions to get started. I've tried to keep them as simple and time-effective as possible. (See Appendix D for U.S. to metric conversions.)

Because this is a book of magick, I've chosen to set up the rest of the book topically so you can look at a variety of potential recipes to meet whatever need you have. This will allow you to choose something you find meaningful and pleasing to your taste buds. And to help you personalize the recipes, lists of potential alternative ingredients are included in the beginning of each section.

Finally, in Appendix C of this book I've included a list of some beverages that were sacred to various gods and goddesses. This list is designed for those of you who may be thinking about making a beverage libation, or one suited to an offering on your altar. This way you can design the beverage to please the Divine, and hopefully your palate too!

Cheers!

ABUNDANCE AND PROSPERITY

"To rejoice in the prosperity of another is to partake in it."
—W. Austin

Who of us couldn't use a little extra abundance in our lives? Mind you, this abundance can come in many forms, from a profuse garden to increased financial flow. It can also mean abundant joy, abundant health, an abundance of good friends, and other wonderful things that we treasure. So, in making this type of beverage, it's important to focus on exactly what type of plenty you're seeking and then adjust the recipes accordingly.

For example, you might add more green-colored items to a brew for financial prosperity because the western world associates that color with our paper money. Besides drinking this beverage, you could dab a bit on your wallet like a charm to attract more cash, and to keep what you have close by! On the other hand, a brew for a flourishing garden might be better made with the soil in mind, and poured out to the land where it can do the most good!

Here's a list of ingredients commonly associated with this type of energy to refer to for adapting or tweaking your recipes to suit personal tastes and needs:

alfalfa sprouts	ginger	kiwi
almond flavoring	berries	orange juice
banana	grapes	basil
mint	dill	grains
nutty flavoring	tea	tomato juice
lavender	rhubarb	cranberry
green beverages	apple	

You may also wish to consider making these brews during a waxing moon and stirring them clockwise so abundance grows.

Bountiful Beer

2 handfuls dandelion leaves and roots, freshly picked	4 stalks rhubarb
2 lbs. cane sugar	1 gal. water
1/2 oz. beer yeast	1 tsp. ground gingerroot

Directions: All the ingredients for this, except the yeast should be placed in a large pan and boiled for one hour. When this is finished, allow to cool to lukewarm, adding the yeast, which has been suspended in warm water. Bottle after 24 hours, sealed tightly. Drink in three to 40 days without spoilage.

Magickal Associations: Nature's abundance, providence, the harvest.

History/Lore: A favorite farmers beer, prepared from items readily given from a bountiful land. Sometimes nettles, a vegetable that tastes like spinach and is similarly high in iron, were also added for nutritional value.

Berry Orange Harvest

1 lb. cranberries, ground	2 whole seedless oranges, ground
3 1/2 cups sugar	2 cups rum

Directions: Place all your ingredients, including any juice from the grinding process, into a two-quart jar with a secure lid. Keep in a cool area, shaking thoroughly once a day for the next six weeks. Strain into bottles and seal for use over the holidays.

Magickal Associations: The harvest, thankfulness, prosperity.

History/Lore: This beverage is excellent to make with leftovers from the Thanksgiving table, which are already blessed with the energies of gratitude for Divine providence.

Alternatives: Reduce orange by one, adding two peeled ground apples in its place. Magickally this encourages improved wisdom with one's resources so you have what you need when you need it.

Or you can just enjoy some cranberry-orange juice as a non-alcoholic substitute.

Prosperity Persuasion

1 1/2 cups diced broccoli	6 stalks celery
6 large brussels sprouts	6 scallions
1 sprig parsley	1 ltr. water
1 cup chopped asparagus	1 ltr. vodka
salt and pepper to taste	

Directions: Finely chop all your ingredients, placing them in a large pan with water over a medium flame. Allow the vegetables to simmer for about two and a half to three hours until almost mushy in texture. Strain this through a sieve, pressing the vegetable remnants with a wooden spoon to extract juices. Keep the vegetable pieces for a soup base and return the liquid to the pan, mixing in the vodka. Taste the mixture to see if any spices or sugar are necessary for personal enjoyment. Bottle and age one to two months before using.

Magickal Associations: Abundance, good fortune, success.

History/Lore: The color of this beverage turns out to be a luscious green to help encourage growth or improve finances. Serve with a stick of fresh celery.

Alternative: Eliminate the vodka, increase the water by one liter, and simply chill this like you would any vegetable blend.

Harvest Horn

2 cups white grape juice
2 cups apple juice
1 bottle mixed fruit wine
1 orange, sliced

1 cup berries (any)
2 cups ginger ale
grape bunches

Directions: Mix the juices with the wine, adding sliced orange and berries. Allow this to sit at room temperature for 30 minutes, then chill. Add ginger ale when pouring into a punch bowl. Garnish sides of the bowl with grape bunches.

Magickal Associations: Abundance, providence, gathering natural bounty, gratefulness.

History/Lore: The horn of plenty appears in various forms in a diversity of folklore as an object that pours divine goodness unceasingly—usually in the form of foods or blessings.

Serving idea: If you have some readily available, the magick of this beverage is accentuated by serving it in a drinking horn instead of a glass. You can substitute non-alcoholic wine without loosing any symbolic value.

Money Punch

2 cups dark rum
1 cup Kahlua
2 tsp. sugar
1 orange, sliced
1 1/2 qts. orange coffee

2 medium cinnamon sticks
4 whole cloves
3/4 tsp. nutmeg
1 whole almond per person

Directions: Place rum, Kahlua, and sugar together in a large heat-proof serving bowl. Light the liquid, using the coffee to extinguish it slowly. This allows the entire mixture to reach your guests warm. Add spices, float orange slices on top, and allow mixture to sit until it reaches a comfortable sipping temperature. Serve in cups garnished with one almond each.

Magickal Associations: Wealth, abundance, resources.

History/Lore: All the spices, nuts, and fruits in this recipe have been chosen for their money-attracting attributes. Oranges were a symbol of prosperity in the Middle Ages due to their high import cost.

Green Abundance

1 cup diced broccoli	2 stalks celery
4 brussels sprouts	3 scallions
1 sprig parsley	1 cup asparagus
1 cup tomato juice	1 cup alfalfa sprouts
(or 2 whole tomatoes)	salt and pepper to taste

Directions: Follow basic recipe in Chapter 2 for juicing.

Magickal Associations: Abundance, good fortune, success.

History/Lore: Asparagus was thought to be one of Julius Caesar's favorite foods, contributing to his strength, and celery was used in Rome to prevent hangovers. In this case, the color of this beverage is a rich green to help encourage growth or improved finances. Visualize your needs while you drink!

Cacao Cash

2 oz. sweet baker's chocolate	1 oz. unsweetened chocolate
2 Tbsp. milk	1/2 stick cinnamon
1 Tbsp. sugar	1/2 tsp. vanilla
1 beaten egg	nutmeg and heavy cream (garnish)

Directions: Slowly melt the chocolate with milk and cinnamon over a double boiler. Stir in the sugar and vanilla until sugar is fully dissolved. Turn off the heat and fold in the beaten (to frothy) egg and serve with a bit of cream and cinnamon floating on top.

Magickal Associations: Improving finances, abundance, getting your money's worth.

History/Lore: In Mexico, the beans of the cacao tree were used as currency, and only the rich could afford to drink beverages made from them, quite literally drinking wealth! Apparently this idea was not unique to Mexico as it has similar versions in ancient Mesopotamia, and even among the Aztecs.

Alternatives: Try orange chocolate in place of the baker's for similar magickal effects, or mint chocolate to help heal a financially stressful situation.

Cafe L'Orange

6 cups strong orange coffee
6 cups hot chocolate
1 tsp. vanilla extract
cinnamon

6 slices fresh orange, peeled
1 cup heavy cream
orange peel

Directions: In each cup place one orange slice, pouring over equal quantities of hot cocoa and freshly brewed coffee. Mingle vanilla extract with heavy cream. Then, top cocoa/coffee mixture with cream, grated orange peel, and cinnamon.

Magickal Associations: Prosperity, abundance, accomplishment.

History/Lore: In the Middle Ages, oranges were a very rare and costly commodity to most European homes, and as such were used frugally or to show off ones wealth. Magickally speaking, this precious association slowly attached itself with the fruit even after it was readily available.

Alternative: This beverage is often enjoyed in Belgium, but sometimes cinnamon takes place of hot cocoa with a dash of orange extract.

BALANCE

"... according to the symmetry of their [atoms] shapes and sizes and positions and order, and they remain together thus the coming into being of complex things is affected."
—Simplicius, *De Caelo*

Learning to balance our day-to-day life with spirituality is one of the most important steps to magickal mastery. Even as atoms balance themselves into a harmony to make something greater, that is what our magickal energy does. And in times that are terribly hectic, we also need to learn symmetry between work, home, play, and other activities that are necessary to a healthy, happy outlook. Consequently, in making these beverages, try to keep everything even—each herb should be measured the same, each juice poured out in the same amount. Remember that symbolism here is just as important as your ingredients. Maybe even look for a yin/yang styled cup from which to drink!

It is difficult to provide an ingredient list for these beverages because much depends on your area of need. However, generally speaking the herb cumin and the color purple (perhaps grape juice) help with this type of effort, as do the stones onyx and fluorite, which may be used to create a crystal tincture. Garnish your cup with an oak leaf for a little more symmetry.

In terms of timing, you may wish to consider making these brews at noon or midnight, dusk or dawn, the traditional in-between times that hover on the edge of beginnings and endings. In choosing the exact time, consider what it is you're trying to balance out. For example, if you need to strengthen your conscious mind so that your emotions don't overwhelm sound thinking, noon would be a good choice because sunlight accents that part of our nature.

Symmetry's Simmering

2 pints water	4 oz. sugar
6 oranges, juiced	2 pints rum
1 tsp. whole cloves	2 whole cinnamon sticks
1 tsp. whole allspice berries	

Directions: Mix the juice of oranges with the two pints water in a quart-sized pan. Warm over low flame with spices and sugar until a tea-like consistency is reached. Add rum and serve with pieces of cinnamon stick. Makes one quart.

Magickal Associations: Balance, fruitfulness, symmetry, and abundance.

History/Lore: The orange tree is unique in that it bears its leaves, flowers, and fruits all at the same time, making it an excellent symbol of bounty and the triune nature of both gods and humankind.

Alternatives: For a purifying beverage, substitute the juice of four lemons for the oranges.

Temperance Tonic

1 pint peppermint schnapps	1 tsp. chamomile
3 bay leaves	4 dandelion heads
1/2 cup crushed blackberries	1/2 tsp. golden seal
1/2 tsp. catnip leaves	1/4 tsp. sage
1/2 tsp. tansy	1/2 tsp. yarrow
1 cup honey	

Directions: Warm the schnapps over a low flame with honey and blackberries until they are fully mixed in. Meanwhile, wrap your herbs in a double thickness of gauze or cheesecloth. This bundle will be suspended in the schnapps, once cooled to luke-warm, for three months (sealed tightly). Strain before using. For a lighter beverage, mix with equal amounts of water and serve hot.

Magickal Associations: Moderation, self-control, and regulation.

History/Lore: Most all-purpose tonics are regarded as anything that can improve energy, physical strength, or provide nourishment in order to bring balance back to the body. This recipe combines the traditional tonic herbs into a syrup-like composition to take in teaspoonfuls either in the morning or at night.

Yin/Yang Zinger

6 lemons, peeled	6 limes, peeled
1 lb. sugar (or honey)	2 qts. water

Directions: Save the peels of three lemons and limes, from which the white pith has been removed. Place the peels in a large pot, covered with one qt. boiling water, and allow to sit and infuse like a tea. Meanwhile, express the juice of all six lemons and limes, adding the remainder of the water, sugar, and the juice from the peels. Taste to see if additional sweetening is required, then serve over ice.

Magickal Associations: Equilibrium. Also useful in cleansing and protection.

History/Lore: Lemon and lime are perfect balance points to each other in color, flavor, and energy. Lemon juice is often used to help purge magickal tools of unwanted energies, and lime is considered an effective protection against negative magick.

Heart-Head Symmetry

1 small bundle of lilac petals
2 tsp. lavender
1 tsp. chopped violet petals
1 1/2 cups carbonated water
1 white rose (no leafs or green parts)
2 tsp. pennyroyal
sweetener to taste

Directions: For this recipe, it will be necessary to infuse your floral essence before adding it to the carbonated water. For this, simply add the flower petals, once cleaned, to a cup of warm (not boiling) water and allow to simmer until their coloration is all but gone. Cool this mixture and add enough so that your soda has the lovely bouquet of fresh blossoms.

Magickal Associations: Harmony, accord, balanced relationships, and communication, especially among families or groups.

History/Lore: All the flowers chosen for this recipe are strongly associated with the energy of agreement and compatibility.

BANISHMENT

"Away from me, all negativity; forever to stay... away! away!"
—Loresinger, Incantation

Banishment is a very ancient art based on the idea that magick is to turn and change, and what better thing to be turning away from ourselves than negative energy? With that in mind, in making your banishing brews you need to be asking yourself whether the source of the difficulty is internal or external. Do you need to change something of yourself, or something that's coming from outside and disrupting the harmony of your life? Upon answering that question, you can drink your potion for internal transformation, or pour it out to wash away negativity.

Here are some of the ingredients associated with banishing:

basil	clove	cumin
garlic	leek	lilac
mint	onion	peach
pepper	rosemary	sloe berries
wintergreen	anise	sage
woodruff	apple	cinnamon

Unlike many of the beverages discussed herein, these types of brews are best made during a waning moon and stirred counterclockwise because your goal is that of decreasing. If you happen to work during an eclipse, all the better—in this instance the moon figuratively disappears, making a strong symbol upon which to direct your focus. Most people consider the color of banishing to be black, so for internal work you may wish to use a black-colored drinking vessel.

Negativity Nemesis

1 qt. warm apple wine freshly
2 oz. sugar
1/4 pint water
stick cinnamon

1/2 cup woodruff flowers
picked
slice of orange per glass

Directions: Allow the woodruff to set in the warm wine for a half hour, then remove. To this add sugar and water. This serves about six people and may be prepared warm or cold. Garnish with orange slices and cinnamon.

Magickal Associations: Victory, protection, banish negativity.

History/Lore: In Germany, woodruff is called "the master of the woods," with a rich smell similar to that of cinnamon. Its white flowers are sacred to the Goddess and it has often been used in magick to protect against impishness.

Alternative: Substitute apple juice or cider for the wine.

Run Away Red!

3 1/2 lbs. currants (red)	3 lbs. sugar
1 raspberry tea bag	1/4 lb. raisins
1/4 orange sliced	1/3 pkg. (1/4 oz.) yeast
1 gal. water	

Directions: Place your cleaned currants in a large bucket with orange slices. Heat one half of the water to boiling and pour it over the berries. While hot, crush the fruit, then leave the mixture to set covered for two days. Strain thoroughly. Move the currant juice to the stove adding remaining water and sugar. Bring to a simmer stirring constantly until the sugar is dissolved. Follow as with basic recipe, allowing four days of open air fermentation. When you strain this mixture again for bottling, place three raisins in the bottom of each vessel, then age.

Magickal Associations: Turning away unwanted spirits or devas.

History/Lore: This wine turns a beautiful bright red color, of which certain mischievous spirits and fairy folk are said to be afraid.

Banishing Winter Blues

1 handful each pansy and borage flowers	4 cups water, warm
	juice of one lemon
sugar to taste	

Directions: Leave the pansy and borage flowers in warm water for 12 hours to infuse. Strain, adding lemon juice and sweetener. Garnish with a slice of lemon or fresh, cheerful petals.

History/Lore: Borage has often been thought to sooth the melancholy that can come after long, arduous winters. Pansy is known by the alternative folk name "hearts ease" and is likewise felt beneficial to restore ones wits. The additional benefit is that this beverage is full of healthful minerals, including calcium.

Solar-Powered Papaya

1 cup papaya juice	1 cup milk
1 tsp. sugar	1 egg white, beaten
4 crushed strawberries	2 Tbsp. honey

Directions: Blend together the papaya juice with milk and sugar. Meanwhile, beat the egg white until frothy. Scoop one heaping tablespoonful on top of the glass. Mash together the strawberries and honey and drizzle in the middle of the egg. Serve chilled.

History/Lore: The visual effect of this drink is not unlike a sun in splendor with yellow rays beneath, and bright red in the center ready to chase away any lingering shadows in your life. In the West Indies, papaya is known as the medicine tree and is rich in vitamin A.

Alternative: Add a dash of cinnamon to increase its potency.

Anti-Magick Brew

4 to 5 figs	1/2 cup raisins
1 cup pearl barley	peel of 1/2 orange
3 cups water	1 slice lemon

Directions: Cook the barley in three cups of water. Strain the resulting liquid onto fruits. Return fruits to the stove, cooking until tender. Squeeze the lemon slice over top of the whole mixture, cool, and strain. Drink only the liquid, preserving the cooked fruit for pie or tarts.

Magickal Associations: Turning undesirable magickal energy away from you.

History/Lore: Barley's earthy quality helps ground out energy, while lemon cleanses.

Spirit Be Gone Brew

1 tsp. raspberry leaf	1 tsp. black currant leaf
1 tsp. lemon balm	1 tsp. valarian
1 tsp. chamomile	4 cups boiling water

Directions: This beverage is prepared like a normal tea.

Magickal Associations: Protection from spirits, purification, quiet restfulness.

History/Lore: The ingredients in this recipe are purported to drive away unwanted ghostly guests. For this purpose, use the tea as an asperging beverage as well as one to consume.

Garlic Protection

1 qt. water	15 cloves garlic
2 bay leaves	2 sprigs fresh sage
1/2 tsp. thyme	1/2 tsp. rosemary
salt and pepper	2 egg yolks
1/3 cup parmesan and romano cheese	1/4 cup olive oil

Directions: Boil water with herbs for 45 minutes, strain. Retain the garlic and press into broth. Meanwhile beat eggs, cheese, and oil slowly together. To the egg mixture, add one cup of broth and beat again. Mix this thoroughly into garlic bouillon base over low heat until thick. Serve with bread crumbs or croutons on top.

Magickal Associations: Banishing, protection from malevolent influences.

History/Lore: Deemed a kind of cure-all, a recipe similar to this is a favorite part of the French Yule celebrations. This beverage has a purgative quality, especially against negative energies.

Violet Safety

2 cups boiling water	1 tsp. dried violets
1 Tbsp. aniseed	1 cup cream
1 tsp. strong, loose black tea	sugar
crushed ice	

Directions: Bundle the aniseed, tea, and dried violets together in a tea ball or gauze bag to steep in the hot water for about 20 minutes or until the water smells heady. Stir in sugar to dissolve, then chill. When cold, add one cup of cream and serve over crushed ice.

Magickal Aspects: Safety, protection from negative magick or malignant spirits, peaceful sleep.

History/Lore: In the time of Virgil, anise was considered a potent means for turning the "evil eye," as well as an effective deterrent to nightmares. Violets were similarly used by the ancient Greeks to bring peaceful sleep and safety from spirits.

Alternatives: Add one teaspoon of chamomile or valerian root if you are making this specifically for sleep. Both herbs have a relaxing effect on nerves. Please note that this beverage can be served hot simply by adding the cream while the tea is still warm and eliminating the ice. If dried violets are not available, try a stick of cinnamon or one teaspoon fennel for similar magickal results.

BEAUTY AND GLAMOURY

"The fountain of beauty is the heart."

—Francis Quarles

Like it or not, we live in a world strongly swayed by external appearances and first impressions. Thankfully witches had an old ally in learning to shift our auric energies to exude an air of confidence and attractiveness: the fairy folk. According to legend, it was they who taught the art of glamoury (of astral illusion) to us.

The modern art of glamoury, however, is not what most people think it to be. What you are doing is creating an atmosphere around yourself versus creating a whole different appearance. Unlike the movies, your hair color won't change, and makeup won't suddenly appear. Instead, the way people feel around you and how they interpret that feeling changes to mirror the energy you've put into your aura through the brew.

Here are some of the edible ingredients commonly associated with beauty. For a crystal tincture, amber is recommended.

avocado	lovage	egg
ginseng	oats	primrose
heather	lavender	beet juice
nut milks	cream	

On a personal note, I like creating these when the moon is full, or when candles are gleaming, because both sources of light do wonders for most people's skin. Additionally, I like to use soda pop as a base for some of these creations because it sparkles, just as we want our auras to gleam with magick.

Bear in mind, however, that magickal glamoury is a temporary coping mechanism. It definitely stresses the positive, but shouldn't be employed with those you care deeply about, or when you're in your own space. Those are times to be wholly yourself, without flash and fanfare.

Courage Cordial

1 ltr. vodka	1 cup maple syrup
2 cups pecans, ground	2 cups almonds, ground

Directions: Warm the vodka slightly with maple syrup so that the syrup mixes completely with it. Meanwhile, place the nuts in a wide-mouth container (with lid). Pour the warm vodka mixture over top and seal tightly. Leave in a dark, breezy place and shake daily for eight weeks, then strain and enjoy.

Magickal Associations: Personal changes, reversing cycles, modifying habits, seeing yourself in a positive light.

History/Lore: The number eight (months) is the number of change. Additionally, the ingredients here are all aligned with the Air element to encourage the winds to bring a refreshing metamorphosis in your outlooks and demeanor, projecting a more comely air.

Alternatives: Replace vodka with one liter of water and increase syrup to three cups, adding wine yeast as directed in the wine chapter. This produces a lovely golden beverage with lower alcohol content.

Creamy Beauty

2 beaten eggs	2 qts. milk
1 lemon, peeled	1 qt. cream
4 cups brandy	1 cup sugar

Directions: Place beaten eggs and milk in a sauce pan and stir. Carefully remove as much white pith from the lemon peel as possible, then shred and place with milk mixture. Slowly warm, adding sugar, until the liquid almost boils, then remove from heat, immediately removing lemon. Slowly add brandy and cream, beating the whole with a wire whisk until frothy. Serve in a punch bowl with whipped cream, if desired.

Magickal Associations: Glamoury, lunar/goddess energy, and attractiveness.

History/Lore: The Gaelic word for milk translates to mean heart, and in this case we are taking to heart the idea of beauty starting within. Additionally, the phrase "creamy white skin" has often been associated with beauty. We are simply applying the symbolic value differently by using the cream to create this beverage.

Tropical Temptation

16 oz. pineapple juice	1 gal. water
2 cups coconut	3 lbs. sugar
1 8-oz. can mandarin oranges	1/3 pkg. yeast
1 large ripe banana	2 cups papaya juice
5 kiwi fruit, peeled and diced	

Directions: Follow basic wine directions, making sure to boil this beverage before cooling for yeast. The boiling process helps to incorporate the differently weighted fruit juices. Shake daily during fermentation and strain well.

Magickal Associations: Glamoury to improve approachability and appeal.

History/Lore: The fruits of warm regions offer a refreshing change from apples and grapes. In Honduran legend, it was the banana leaf that covered Adam and Eve, not fig or apple. Pineapple is the fruit of welcome, and coconut figures in beautifying efforts.

Oriental Rose

1 orange, sliced and seeded (no pith)	1 Tbsp. malt extract
2 capfuls rose water	1 tsp. sugar or honey
4 oz. orange soda	4 oz. skim milk

Directions: Place your ingredients together in a blender, first on low speed to dice the orange finely. Then turn to high until an orange-white foam is forming on top. Serve over crushed ice.

Magickal Associations: Self-confidence, feeling upbeat and looking as good as you feel. Also physical health.

History/Lore: Oranges played an integral role in offerings to the gods of the East, being a very valued commodity thought to provide joy and abundance to all who receive them. Rose water promotes self-love and sound judgment.

Pink Personality

2 pink grapefruit	1 orange
1 banana	1 cup strawberries
1 cup raspberries	honey or sugar to taste
1 cup soda water	

Directions: Juice and strain fruits before adding honey or soda water. Mix thoroughly.

Magickal Associations: Overall well-being, exuding an air of friendliness and approachability.

History/Lore: I have used the combination of color (pink) here with the natural love-energies of the berries in this drink to produce a beverage that encourages good thoughts about self and others.

CHANGE AND TRANSFORMATION

"Today is not yesterday—We ourselves change. How then, can our works and thoughts, if they are always to be the fittest, continue always the same?"

—Thomas Carlyle

Change is one of the few constants upon which we can depend, as much of a dichotomy as that may seem to be! Additionally, magick is designed to be a transformer, something that shifts energy into more positive patterns. Brews for change are one way to help us accomplish this, at least in part because of the changes that happen just from the normal preparation process!

Cooking has transformation at its heart—you take one thing and make it into another. So realistically, any ingredient can become the key component for transformational tonics, depending on what you hope to change! Want to turn failure into success? Try grape juice laden with bay. To turn weakness into strength, use mead with thyme. The key is knowing the symbolism behind your ingredients.

There are a few items, under the influence of Saturn, that in themselves inspire change. These include vinegar, beet, and quince. You will sometimes see vinegar used in beverage, but usually those for health, so I might suggest this as a libation or anointing ingredient over one to quaff. Also, if your transformation tonics can themselves change form during the creation process, all the better! For example, adding finely crushed ice to a beverage gives it a semi-solid, shapable consistency. The alteration in form visually stresses the change you're making internally.

Because of the diversity of options, I've decided to focus on specific types of change in this section. Just alter your ingredients to better suit the transitions you face.

Chocolate Mood Lifter

2 oz. semi-sweet chocolate	1/2 cup cold water
1/2 cup sugar	1 cup heavy cream, whipped
1/2 qt. milk	1/2 ltr. mint liqueur

Directions: Place the chocolate in a sauce pan with water and stir over low heat until totally melted and mixed. Add to this the sugar, cooking about 10 minutes until thickened. Let this cool, folding in the whipped cream. Set aside. Next heat the milk over a low flame until lukewarm. Add the mint liqueur and cream mixture, stirring until all is well incorporated. Enjoy hot, or store in the refrigerator, shaking before serving.

Magickal Associations: Pleasure, warmth, fanciful diversions, turning a negative perspective into something more positive.

History/Lore: Pre-Columbian civilizations in South America were known to cultivate chocolate. Mexican chocolate was imported to the New World first as a delicacy, and later as an important baking staple.

Alternatives: For a beverage to encourage "sun" energies and health alongside enjoyment, use orange-flavored liqueur in this recipe in place of the mint. If the mint liqueur is too expensive, use vodka instead and add a teaspoon of mint extract to the chocolate-water mixture while it is melting.

Fire Refinement

2 large tomatoes	2 cloves garlic
2 red peppers	1 cup chopped red cabbage
1 tsp. lime juice	1 tsp. hot sauce
4 cups water	1 ltr. whiskey

Directions: Place all your ingredients, finely chopped, into a large pan with water. Simmer for two hours over low flame. Strain the mixture through a sieve, pressing as much juice as possible out of the vegetables. Mix with whiskey and bottle, aging for at least 30 days before use.

Magickal Associations: Purification, drastic change, Fire and Sun related magick.

History/Lore: This beverage, very appropriate to summer observances, uses the traditional herbs, plants, and colors of fire to ignite transformation in your life.

Metamorphosis Punch

5 cups sugar or honey	2 lemons sliced
1 1/2 liter of water	2 or 3 whole cloves
1 cup wine vinegar	1 pint mint liqueur
3 Tbsp. dried mint	

Directions: Bring the sugar and water to boil until the sugar is completely dissolved. To this add vinegar, mint, clove, and lemons. Simmer for 20 minutes. Strain and serve chilled. Mix with liqueur.

Magickal Associations: Refinement, well-being, poise, personal change.

History/Lore: A version of an ancient Persian beverage considered to be very healthful, this drink gets its magickal potency from the Greek story of Pluto and Persephone. Persephone, in a moment of jealous rage, crushed the nymph Minthe under her foot. Pluto, in sadness, transformed her into one of the most favored herbs of history with a gentle, sweet smell.

Maple Modifications

4 gal. water	1 qt. maple syrup
2 cups hop	1 pkg. yeast

Directions: A nice, simple recipe, your water, syrup, and hops are brought to a low rolling boil for about 20 minutes. Strain and allow to cool before adding suspended yeast. This needs to sit for another 24 hours, be strained again, then bottled. Ready in one week.

Magickal Associations: Tapping inner wells, centering, peaceful transitions.

History/Lore: The maple leaf, having three distinct sections, is representative of the three-fold nature of both God and humankind. Each aspect of these is bound together in a smooth stream (the syrup) that gives attention to the whole person to encourage balance.

Alternatives: Any berries added to this beverage will help encourage self-love to bring well-being.

Strawberries of Virtue

8 whole strawberries
1 cup raspberries

2 cups orange juice
1 cup crushed ice

Directions: Place all ingredients together in a blender, adding more ice if you desire a thicker beverage. Sweetener is not usually needed.

History/Lore: While berries are generally considered a love food, we have to love ourselves before we can really incorporate new qualities and positive changes into our lives. The orange is for a healthy outlook!

Alternative: It is nice to garnish this drink with carnation, which symbolizes pride in your progress.

Freedom Fountain

1/2 cup peach juice
1/2 tsp. apple extract
sweetener to taste

1 1/2 cups carbonated water
dash anise
1 bay leaf (garnish)

Directions: Follow the basic soda pop recipe, placing a large bay leaf on the side of the glass. This is best accomplished by splitting it up the middle and sliding it over the rim.

Magickal Associations: Breaking bondage, changing bad habits, personal transformation.

History/Lore: According to cunning folk, peaches help to rid negativity and improve wisdom while apple encourages healing, anise increases awareness, and the bay leaf is an icon of strength.

CLEANSING AND PURIFICATION

"So great is the effect of cleanliness upon man, that it extends even to his moral character."

—Benjamin Rumford

Cleanliness is not simply a physical state; it has a psychic and astral application too. You will sometimes hear about people who have poor spiritual hygiene. This means that they don't control energy very well, and often leave bits of negativity and raw emotion laying around. This is very irresponsible in that those who consequently stumble over the negativity end up feeling out of sorts and disarmed by the energy. So it remains for each of us to become our own priest/ess, and begin regular cleansing and purification rites.

What does this mean exactly? Well, in part it means cleansing and purifying your body, mind, and spirit on a routine basis. It also means doing likewise for your sacred space of home. Purifying beverages can help us accomplish both tasks, in that the ingredients will have purgative qualities for both consumption or asperging

Here are some of the ingredients commonly used as magickal purifiers and cleansers:

anise	bay	chamomile
coconut	fennel	lavender
lemon	mint	sage
thyme	valerian	grapefruit
lime	water	orange
pepper	vinegar	honey
cinnamon	rosemary	onion
beer	salt	white beverages
rum	garlic	

Purification and cleansing might be best done during the dark moon (at the same time we traditionally weed the garden to keep those nasty things out!). For crystal tinctures use aquamarine.

Purifying Beer

4 qts. boiling water
1 cup sugar
raisins (optional)

1 lemon, sliced and seeded
1/8 oz. beer yeast

Directions: Turn the flame off below the boiling water and add sliced lemons and sugar. Cover to let cool until lukewarm. Meanwhile, dissolve the yeast in 1/4 cup warm water and let it stand. Pour this into the pot, stirring once, then allow to age overnight (a full 24 hours) until bubbles form on the surface. Strain this into your bottles. If desired, add a raisin to each bottle. Chill before serving. This recipe has a short shelf life and is ready to consume immediately. After two or three weeks it will become too bitter to drink, but can instead be mixed with brown sugar to make a sweet-and-sour glaze for poultry.

Magickal Associations: Purification, cleansing, refreshed love and ideas.

History/Lore: Lemon brings zest and active energy to any beverage. Because it has a natural purgative quality, it is mostly associated with magick for refinement. Lemon rind has also been frequently used in love sachets and potions.

Alternative: Substitute 1 1/2 lbs. of currants for the lemons in this recipe and reduce your sugar by one cup for a beer empowered for protection and fire magick.

Absolution Wine

1/2 lb. onions
1 lb. raisins
2 lbs. sugar
  (3 for more sweetness)

1/2 lb. potatoes
1 gal. water
1/2 pkg. yeast

Directions: Peel and slice onions, placing them in a large pot. Do likewise with the potatoes, then add the raisins, diced. In a separate container, warm water and sugar together until dissolved, pouring this over the onion-potato mixture. Next add yeast after you have suspended it in 1/4 cup warm water. Leave this to ferment in a warm place with a loose cover for two weeks. Strain and bottle. Generally this is a dry wine, with no residual onion scent.

Magickal Associations: Cleansing prior to religious study and worship, foresight, abundance.

History/Lore: Egyptians worshiped onions, regarding them as one of their most important foods. Hindus likewise felt the onion to be most significant, making it into a symbol of religious mystery and an object of divination. Arabic and Chinese people used onions to ward off magick, and in many herbals onion juice is recommended as a purgative.

Alternative: Barley may be used in place of potatoes for improved providence (same proportion).

Rum and Citrus Cleansing

12 ripe grapefruits
1 gal. water
1/2 pkg. sparkling yeast
1 ltr. dark rum
4 lbs. dark honey

Directions: Pour water into large pot. Peel your grapefruits, carefully removing the white pith from the peels and the fruit itself. Cut up peels from four of the fruits and place in a large pot with the sectioned fruit itself. Bring to a low rolling boil for 20 minutes, then cool. Strain the fruit, juicing carefully, then return the liquid to the pan to add honey. Boil again for 15 minutes to clear residue, then follow as with basic recipe for mead. After three months of aging, strain the base liquid again, testing for sweetness, and add rum along with any additional honey you feel is necessary for flavor. Age for a minimum of six months.

Magickal Associations: Purification, knowledge, health.

History/Lore: In some rural areas of England, the grapefruit is still called "forbidden fruit" as it is one of many to be thought to be the actual fruit of Eden. Additionally, the tart yellow juice has a cleansing, protective nature.

Alternatives: For richer flavor, try adding one can of frozen grapefruit or pineapple juice at the same time as the honey.

Pink Grapefruit Wash

2 qts. fresh strawberries	8 cups sugar
4 pink grapefruit (large)	1 slice lemon
1 lb. seedless raisins	1/3 pkg. wine yeast
1 black tea bag	

Directions: Juice your grapefruit, extracting as much liquid as possible. Place this in a large container with raisins and water, then leave overnight in a warm area. Move this kettle to the stove, adding strawberries, the tea bag, sugar, and lemon. Follow basic cooking recipe as given above except that you should allow cloth-covered fermentation for six days before straining off berries and raisins. This will allow a fuller-flavored wine.

After first fermentation, wine should be allowed to set for four months before another straining, then aged an additional six months before serving.

Magickal Associations: Cleansing outmoded outlooks and improving attitudes.

History/Lore: While strawberries are a traditional love fruit, the light pink coloration of this wine turns its energy more toward matters of self-awareness. The grapefruit cleanses unwanted energy.

Refining Ginger

1/2 cup maple syrup (real)	1 qt. water
1" bruised gingerroot	1 pt. ginger liqueur
1/4 cup white vinegar	1 tsp. anise seed

Directions: Warm the water, gingerroot, anise, and maple syrup together until they are fully blended. Remove ginger slices. To this, add all other ingredients in a glass pitcher, stirring well. Chill.

Magickal Associations: Cleansing, purification, health, and vital energies.

History/Lore: Beverages like this were common among early German settlers to America, especially those who did a lot of hay harvesting, which often left the throat and sinuses raw. It's very effective for getting rid of allergy itches.

Alternatives: Instead of using ginger liqueur, for a non-alcoholic alternative substitute one pint of bergamot tea (such as Earl Grey) for similar magickal energies.

Pineapple Purity

5 cups orange juice   3 cups pineapple juice
1 slice of lemon, squeezed   1 vanilla cookie stick
orange whipped cream (garnish)

Directions: Pour orange, pineapple, and squeezed lemon juice into a large covered container and shake well. For simple purification rites nothing else should be added. For dessert, however, I recommend a teaspoon of sugar, a gourmet vanilla cookie, and some orange whipped cream to garnish it.

Magickal Associations: Cleansing, health, psychic and physical purification, change.

History/Lore: This drink is an excellent prelude to a ritual fast or bath, both of which have purgative qualities. In the case of the latter, I suggest adding lemon, orange, and pineapple rinds to the water.

Alternatives: Lime, mint, and guava juice can be substituted for lemon, orange, and the vanilla cookie. In this case, the mint leaf is used for garnish, the magickal effect being much the same.

Purification Pottage

1 tsp. anise   1 tsp. lavender
1 bay leaf   1 tsp. lemon juice
1 tsp. chamomile   1 tsp. mint
1 tsp. fennel   1 tsp. rosemary
1 tsp. thyme

Directions: Add all the above to a tea kettle of hot water. Steep for 15 minutes, then serve piping hot before meditation.

History/Lore: The herbs for this tea were chosen for their cleansing effect on both the body and psyche.

Alternative: To increase the effect of this tea specifically for divination efforts, add a slice of orange and a bit of onion to the stew. This tastes a little like a weak soup.

COMMUNICATION

"Brandy must be a decoction of hearts and tongues, because after drinking it I fear nothing and I talk wonderfully."
—James G. Frazer

One of the most difficult things for most people is determining the difference between what's heard and what someone actually meant by their words. In days when our language forms and slang change nearly as quickly as socks, there is a tremendous need to develop our spiritual ears to hear truly. Likewise our words need to be sensitive, honest, and filled with magick. How can this be accomplished?

The nice part about magickal beverages is that the first place they touch is our lips and tongues. Also, you have the option of making gargles out of your brews, to refresh your mouth and words with the energy needed at the moment! Here's a list of ingredients commonly associated with communication skills:

brandy	mead	yellow hues
dandelion	mint	sage
clove	honey	raspberries

In terms of crystal tinctures, you can combine agate, beryl, bloodstone, and carnelian for the greatest effect. Bless your brews while standing in the eastern quarter of a magickal circle, the region associated with effective conveying of messages.

Cordial Cordial!

1 cup water	1 Tbsp. vanilla extract
1 whole clove	1 small cinnamon stick
1 cup heather honey	2 cups vodka

Directions: Place the water in a large saucepan and bring to a low rolling boil. Add spices, allowing to infuse like a tea while the water cools. If you don't like cloves that much, remove them before the water reaches lukewarm. Strain, then re-warm to dissolve the honey, removing any froth that comes to the surface. Add vodka, strain, and bottle securely, allowing to age for two weeks before consumption.

Magickal Associations: Messages, rapport, opening the lines of discourse.

History/Lore: This beverage, with but minor changes, owes its origins to Prussia, where it is believed to aid smooth speech and effective communications. Cloves were a favorite medieval breath freshener used between lovers who hoped to steal a kiss!

Alternatives: To further accentuate the power of speech in this recipe, try replacing the vanilla with either mint or almond extract. Both of these are aligned with the element of Air, which helps move messages towards their proper destination.

The Messenger

1 lb. fresh raspberries	1 lb. fresh blackberries
1 16-oz. can frozen	1 gal. water
raspberry-cranberry juice	2 lbs. light honey
1/2 pkg. yeast	1/2 ltr. raspberry brandy
1/2 ltr. blackberry brandy	

Directions: This recipe is prepared the same as the Rum and Citrus Cleansing (p. 85), except that you do not strain out the raspberries until just before you add the brandy. The leftover fruit makes excellent conserves when mixed with coconut and apple plus six cups sugar, and boiled.

Magickal Associations: Sending and receiving messages, including those directed to the God/dess.

History/Lore: The blackberry has the unique distinction of being regarded as the burning bush of biblical fame. In the Americas, certain Native American tribes used blackberries mixed with honey as ceremonial food. The raspberry was similarly honored among the Native Americans with a special ceremony upon their first harvest where they would ask the spirit of the fruit for help with all endeavors of peace and war, especially communication.

Alternative: If the price of brandy is prohibitive, try a fruit-flavored vodka in this recipe instead.

Talk-It-Over Brew

4 12-oz. bottles dark ale	1 orange peeled
1/2 cup cognac	nutmeg (garnish)
4 tsp. honey	

Directions: Slowly heat all your ingredients until the honey is well blended, then pour into a warm punch bowl. Sprinkle top with nutmeg and a bit of cinnamon, if desired. Makes enough for eight people.

Magickal Associations: Flowing discourse, free parlay, ease of communications.

History/Lore: In the Elizabethan era, punches similar to this were considered quite able to encourage free speech among the celebrants—to the point of rumor-mongering!

Dandelion Discussions

1 gal. orange juice	1 lemon, juiced
3 cups dandelion petals	1/4 cup of sugar
ginger ale (optional)	

Directions: Clean off the dandelion petals with cool water. In the meantime, warm the orange juice and lemon together, then add dandelions. Make certain you only have petals (no green parts). Add the sugar, stirring constantly until dissolved, strain, and chill. Fill a glass three quarters of the way and add ginger ale to fill for a light, bubbly body.

Magickal Associations: Communicating with the spirit world.

History/Lore: This lovely spring tonic makes good use of pesky weeds to rejuvenate the body with Earth's reawakening. Dandelions are high in vitamins and legends claim that Hecate once entertained Theseus with dandelion water.

Cool-Headed Commentary

1 thinly sliced cucumber   1 qt. tomato juice
1 cinnamon stick   6 whole cloves
salt and pepper to taste

Directions: Mix the spices with juice and cucumber and allow this to set at room temperature for one hour. Remove the spices and chill. Serve with a stalk of celery.

Magickal Associations: Calmness, peace, and tranquility, especially when trying to relay difficult ideas.

History/Lore: The power of the aphorism "cool as a cucumber" in this recipe is undeniable. Actually, cool cucumbers have been used to relieve pain, especially for headaches, in folk medicine, which could have lead to the idea that they ease stress.

Arrowroot Armistice

1 1/2 tsp. arrowroot   1 tsp. superfine sugar
1 cup skim milk

Directions: Mix the arrowroot with a little cold milk and let sit. Boil the remaining milk and pour over the mixture. Return all of this to a small pan, add sugar, and simmer for five minutes. Strain and sweeten, drinking it warm.

Magickal Associations: Courage, especially in discussing difficult relationship issues.

History/Lore: This beverage, known for its calming effect, also acts as lubricant. Sometimes called yarrow, arrowroot when carried by a bride is said to insure seven years of joy and love to the couple.

Alternative: To improve the energies in this beverage specifically for bravery, add one teaspoon of black tea or thyme.

Coffee Talk

2 Tbsp. sugar	1/5 cup water
2 Tbsp. dark coffee beans	

Directions: Begin by grinding the coffee beans to a flour-like powder. In a separate saucepan, stir sugar and water together over low flame until dissolved. Blend in coffee powder and boil. Remove this from the stove heat and let settle. Repeat the boiling process two more times and serve in small cups. Add a twist of lemon rind, nutmeg, cloves, cardamom, or nutmeg for extra flavor.

Magickal Associations: Energy for building friendships and good lines of communication.

History/Lore: This drink is enjoyed popularly in Turkey and Russia with similar reverence to the Arabic coffee house, where friends and associates can gather for light conversation and simple companionship.

CONSCIOUS MIND

"To live so as to keep human consciousness in constant relation with the divine, the spiritual and the eternal, is to individualize the infinite power."

—Mary Baker Eddy

We live in a technologically driven society, which means our conscious, rational self is very important to coping with daily reality. It is also a good helpmate in magick where there is a temptation to let one's heart lead one's head. While magick is an intuitive art, there is a place for logic and clear thinking in our efforts—especially in terms of recognizing our motives, finding a clear, concise method for achieving our goals, and in choosing the tools/ingredients suited to those goals.

Here are some of the common edible components used for stressing and strengthening mental abilities:

coffee	marjoram	mint
nutmeg	rosemary	walnut
celery	caraway	grape
cinnamon	tea	raisins
honey	dill	orange
grapefruit	ginger	coconut
pineapple		

For crystal tinctures, you have amethyst, coral, and fluorite from which to choose. Also, besides drinking your conscious mind brews, you might also consider making them for anointing. Dab a bit on your temples before reading complex materials, or on your books when studying. Put a small drop on the computer screen too!

Conscious Cordial

| 1 cup water | 2 cups sugar |
| 3 cups whiskey | 2 cups mixed orange, lemon, and grapefruit peels |

Directions: Warm the water in a small saucepan with sugar until dissolved. Add this to the whiskey and fruit peels. Please note that you should remove as much of the white lining from the peels as possible to alleviate tartness in this cordial. Leave the ingredients to set together in a sealed container for three months. Strain and serve warm with a touch of honey and cinnamon sticks.

Magickal Associations: Good health, revitalization, refreshed perspectives, mental keenness.

History/Lore: Inhale this beverage deeply to immediately refresh one's conscious mind. Note that this is an excellent blend to offset any colds during the winter months because of its high vitamin C content.

Alternatives: For fruitier flavor and increased vitamin benefit, decrease whiskey by one cup, adding a half cup each orange and grapefruit juice, plus one teaspoon lemon juice. Sugar content may need to be increased for personal taste.

Memory Liqueur

6 12-oz. bottles ginger beer   1/2 cup honey
3 cups ginger ale   1 pt. ginger liqueur
2 oranges sliced thinly   1 sprig fresh rosemary (garnish)

Directions: Use one bottle of ginger beer to warm the honey in until it is dissolved. Add ginger ale to this mixture and stir until well incorporated. Chill remaining ginger beer and liqueur, pouring this with the honey blend into a medium-sized punch bowl. Float oranges on top. May be served hot if desired.

Magickal Associations: Mental health and keenness; energy for memory retention.

History/Lore: Ginger was one of the nine great herbs of the Middle Ages, whereas rosemary is touted as a surefire memory enhancer.

Capable Carnations

1 qt. hot water   1/4 cup lavender
2 cups carnation petals   2 or 3 whole cloves
1 cup sugar   1 stick of cinnamon
1 lemon, peeled   1/2 cup rose petals

Directions: Steep carnation petals, roses, and lavender in water for 24 hours. Strain, then rewarm this liquid adding sugar, lemon peel, cloves, and cinnamon. Simmer for 20 minutes, strain and serve warm.

Magickal Associations: Skill, expertise, mental proficiency

History/Lore: Carnations were the favorite flower of Henry IV of France. Pliny claims that carnations were discovered in Spain during the reign of Augustus Caesar, and recommended them best picked in July. This may be why one of the folk names for carnation is gillyflower (July flower).

Mental Might

1 tsp. grape extract   1/3 tsp. mint extract
1 cup carbonated water   sweetener to taste
mint leaf (garnish)

Directions: Follow general directions for soda pop.

Magickal Associations: The conscious mind; matters of study, education, logic.

History/Lore: Eating grapes is believed to improve concentration and mental faculties. Perhaps that is why the leaders in Rome and Greece were fed them so frequently by servants. Additionally, the aroma of mint is supposed to aid these types of efforts.

Cognizant Tonic

1 bottle dark ale   1/2 tsp. yarrow
1/2 tsp. rosemary   1/2" bruised ginger

Directions: Place rosemary, yarrow, and ginger in a tea ball or gauze covering and steep in the ale, which has been heated. Drink warm with a squeeze of lime or chill and enjoy anytime.

Magickal Associations: Constancy, mental tenacity, courage, especially during troublesome cycles.

History/Lore: According to folk medicine, tonics like this one are excellent for maintaining health, boldness, strength, and mental agility for those trying times.

Sumac Physic

1 generous handful of   1 gal. water
  red staghorn sumac

Directions: Heat water and steep the sumac for 12 hours. Before straining, squeeze the sumac to get as much flavor out as possible. Strain this liquid and sweeten with honey for a lemony-flavored beverage.

Magickal Associations: Sun energy, conscious awareness.

History/Lore: While this recipe is from Morgana's contemporary kitchen, in the 1900s sumac was used as a gargle for sore throat, a tonic for fever, and to ease urinary infections.

Study Strawberries

1 slice orange	1 pt. distilled water
1 whole lemon, juiced	2 tsp. strawberry syrup
1 tsp. vanilla extract	

Directions: Warm the distilled water and orange slice together, adding the juice of one lemon and flavorings. Serve hot.

Magickal Associations: Luck, especially in matters of study or the conscious mind; increased energy.

History/Lore: Recommended mostly for cold symptoms, all the ingredients in this beverage are ruled by Venus, making this an appropriate beverage to bring renewed health to love as well.

DEVOTION AND COMMITMENT

*"There is no bridge so difficult to cross
as the bridge of a broken promise."*
—Hosletter's U.S. Almanac 1897

We normally think of devotion and commitment as having to do with relationships, but these two characteristics have far more dimension than that. What about your devotion to a job, your commitment to a project, or keeping the promise made to a friend? All of these things require a certain level of tenacity and follow-through, which is exactly the type of energy these beverages are designed to inspire.

Some of the edible ingredients that support this goal include:

elderflowers	honey	lemon
orange	tea	violet
rhubarb	figs	peaches

For crystal tinctures use lodestone, which has a natural "stick-to-it" ability! Also, when you're making this particular brew, don't get distracted—really focus on this one! The greater your ability to be "devoted" to the process of making your magickal beverage, the more that energy will filter down into the finished product.

Oath Potion

1/2 lb. dried figs	6 ripe peaches, pitted
6 pomegranates, juiced	1 cup sugar (or more to taste)
1 qt. distilled spirits (your choice)	

Directions: Place your ingredients in equal proportions split between two one-qt. jars. Make sure that peaches and figs are pierced first (use a fork or toothpick). Cover securely, shaking daily for one month, then strain and bottle for use.

Magickal Associations: Commitment, approval, verification.

History/Lore: This beverage is often called Ratafia, and it comes from a tradition of the Middle Ages where parties accepting any legal transaction or agreement would share a drink to celebrate its "ratification." Figs here are used for insight, peaches for wisdom, and pomegranate for luck.

Loyalty Libation

4 lbs. rhubarb, cut	2 lemon rinds, grated
1 gal. boiling water	3 lbs. sugar

Directions: Place the cut rhubarb with lemon rind and sugar in water. Let sit for three days with the pot covered, then strain, returning the liquid to the crock (the rhubarb can be used for pie). Let this stand for two weeks, then place in a large, tightly covered container for one month. Strain and bottle for use.

Magickal Associations: Commitment to relationships, fidelity.

History/Lore: Rhubarb is a plant under the ruling of Venus and the element of Earth, making it an excellent choice for giving any situation requiring personal devotion a strong foundation.

Alternatives: Try decreasing your water content by one quart and substituting apple juice, and adding one cup of raisins with the rhubarb and lemon to the pot. Magickally this is for wisdom in love.

Raspberry Romance

1 cup fresh raspberries   1 cup pineapple juice
1/4 cup grapefruit juice   1 slice of lemon

Directions: Blend or mash the raspberries until very fine. Slowly add the other juices and a touch of sugar if needed to offset any tartness. Garnish with a slice of lemon.

Magickal Associations: Faithfulness, loyalty, and commitment, especially in relationships.

History/Lore: Pineapple juice is thought to hinder stray passions, while berries in general are "love" foods. In some lands, ancient brides carried lemon flowers as a symbol of purity and tenderness.

Tenacity Tonic

1 cup dried jonquil petals   1/2 cup dried French lavender
2 cups warm water   sugar to taste

Directions: Infuse the petals with warm water for 12 hours, preferably during a waxing to full moon. Strain and sweeten. Serve over ice with a fresh flower to bring hope.

History/Lore: In the language of flowers, jonquil means the return of affection, while lavender speaks of appreciation and responsiveness, so that two devoted people may equally give and receive.

Fidelity Brew

2 cups milk   1 sliced onion
1 clove of garlic, minced   1 tsp. butter
1 slice of toast, diced

Directions: Place all ingredients except the toast in your blender, mixing until well incorporated. Warm this over a low flame, add butter, then pour over toast before drinking. This helps relieve chills.

Magickal Associations: Protection of home, relationships, and strong sense of fidelity.

History/Lore: Often used in cold curatives or to improve an appetite. Magickally, Romans were particularly fond of house-leeks (a type of onion) to protect their residence from fire, violence, and the evil eye.

Alternative: Add a cooked potato for a beverage with the thickness of a cream soup.

Rice Integrity

1 oz. rice, rinsed   1/2 qt. water
1/2 qt. milk   lemon peel and nutmeg powder

Directions: Macerate rice for three hours in hot water. Move this to the stove, boiling for one hour then straining the liquid into another saucepan. To this, add milk and boil again, flavoring with lemon and nutmeg.

Magickal Associations: Fidelity in love. New romance, rain magick, fertility.

History/Lore: This beverage is wonderful for easing stomach discomforts and any sense of distrust in relationships.

Mocha Assurance

3 cups Mocha Java coffee   6 Tbsp. strawberry syrup
1 pt. strawberry ice cream

Directions: Prepare coffee as per directions on the label of your grounds. Chill this in the refrigerator until refreshingly cold. Pour three cups of the coffee in a blender with syrup and ice cream for a marvelous shake that cools the body and sweetens disposition.

Magickal Associations: Relief of anxiety, especially in relationships. Energy for renewed trust, accord, and love.

History/Lore: There is nothing that elicits fond, happy memories like going strawberry picking in a wild field. This vision is one of repose and a break from turmoil. Additionally, the strawberry is a love food, making this beverage especially helpful with overactive imaginations or tempers.

DREAMS AND MEDITATIONS

"Children of the night [dreams], of indigestion bred!"
—Charles Churchill

Dream and meditative work is something we're seeing more of in the magickal community. Why? In part as a response to the chaos around us. We need "down" time, moments of soulful stillness where we can hear the Sacred speaking to us, and sort out all the information received by our minds daily.

Now, achieving this is a whole other matter. The chaos does not simply "go away" when we might wish. So we have to find ways to tune out the world and turn our thoughts inward to the dream time and our meditations. The beverages in this section are designed to help you do that. By internalizing their energy, you will have a greater capacity to close yourself off temporarily from any influences other than the spiritual ones you seek.

Here are some of the traditional ingredients associated with dream work and meditation:

marigold	onion	rose
grapes	beer	rosemary
sage	thyme	anise
hops	peppermint	cucumber
carrot		

Consider drinking these beverages out of a silver-toned cup to stress the lunar connection and intuitive self. In terms of timing, I highly recommend a full moon for similar reasons. For best results, drink dream beverages in small quantities prior to going to bed; consume meditation beverages about two hours out so it has time to be internalized. For crystal tinctures turn to moonstone, geodes, and amethyst. Don't forget to dab a bit on your third eye chakra to stress the psychic self's involvement in these processes.

Dreamy Mead

The hops in this recipe are not added as a flavor, but a clarifier that allows the finished mead to be unclouded with a distinctively less dense taste.

1 gal. water	2 oranges
1 oz. cascade hops	1 lemon
4 lbs. light honey	1/2 lb. yellow raisins
1/2 pkg. yeast	

Directions: Place water, hops, honey, and sliced fruit into your pot, boiling as in the basic recipe, but only for 30 minutes. Reduce heat and add chopped raisins, stirring for another five minutes before removing from flame. Cool, strain, and add yeast as instructed above. Place five raisins in each bottle before closing. Aging time after secure corking is one year.

Magickal Associations: Sweet dreams.

History/Lore: A tea made from hops is sometimes used to improve sleep and encourage a healthy appetite.

Devic Nectar

1 qt. apple juice	1 Tbsp. rose water
2 oranges, juiced	1 tsp. thyme
2 cups honey	1 qt. soda
sliced pineapple	sliced lemon
whole grapes	whole cherries
clover flowers (garnish)	

Directions: Place the apple juice, orange juice, honey, rose water, and thyme in a blender and mix well. Pour this into a bowl, slowly adding the soda water. Stir in some ice (about 12 cubes) and float the whole fruits and flowers on top. The amount of whole fruit is according to your personal taste.

Magickal Associations: Understanding and vision of the "unseen" world that come to you in meditations and dreams; fairy friendship and welcoming.

Visionary Vibrancy

2 cups carrot wine
1 cup boiling water
5 whole nutmeg beads

2 cups onion wine
5 pinches (1 tsp.) angelica

Directions: Place the angelica and nutmeg in a tea ball to steep in hot water for 15 minutes. Mix this with the onion and carrot wines, which should be chilled and well blended. Serve to five people on the fifth day of the week for best results.

Magickal Associations: Psychic dreams and spiritual insight.

History/Lore: Five is the number for psychic endeavors, combined powerfully with herbs for spiritual awareness, nutmeg, and angelica. Onions are thought to produce prophetic dreams, and carrots are said to improve vision.

Meditative Mix

1 cup dandelion flowers
1 clove garlic
1 medium onion

2 cups spinach
1 cup romaine lettuce
1 tsp. rose water or
   1/2 cup diced rose petals

Directions: Keep rose water or petals out of juicing process. Add at the end, either by stirring in or floating on top for a garnish.

Magickal Associations: Preparation for meditation, especially those aimed at improving divinatory abilities.

History/Lore: The scent of roses is thought to encourage prophetic dreams. In the language of flowers, the dandelion means "oracle." Garlic is to purify the visions and the green vegetables are for growing awareness.

Dreaming of Love

2 or 3 apples, sliced
1 mint leaf

3 cups hot water
honey and lemon if desired

Directions: Steep the apples and mint together in hot water for one hour, then strain. This is excellent warm with a stick of cinnamon or chilled over ice.

Magickal Associations: Refreshing love. Dreams that teach wisdom and perspective in relationships.

History/Lore: This recipe is favored in France and Australia to help invalids. Additionally, apple is one of the popular ingredients for love potions.

Nutty Notions

2 cups blanched walnuts, crushed	4 thin slices fresh ginger, bruised
1 tsp. black tea	2 cups boiling water
sugar or honey	

Directions: Bring the water to a full rolling boil, then remove from the heat adding all ingredients except sugar. Let mixture sit for 25 minutes. Drain and rewarm, adding sweetening as desired.

Magickal Associations: Resourcefulness and innovation when approaching your dream visions or meditative time.

History/Lore: Nuts are foods for fertility, including improving one's imagination. Meanwhile, ginger adds stimulation and overall energy to your endeavor.

ELEMENTAL AND SEASONAL

"To everything there is a season,
and a time to every purpose under heaven."
—Ecclesiastes 3:1

Witches use the symbolism of the elements (Earth, Air, Fire, and Water), and that of the seasons for many things. First, we use them to honor the Earth's cycles. For example, we might choose to make Air-oriented beverages to serve at Spring gatherings. Second, each of the elements has specific attributes associated with it. By creating a beverage with distinct elemental overtones, we can internalize the energy of that element. For example, if you lacked energy, a Fire-based beverage is a good choice!

Similarly, each season is associated with an element and a location in our sacred circles. Spring corresponds with Air and the East, Summer with Fire and the South, Fall with Water and the West, and Winter with Earth and the North. What does all this mean? Effectively it gives you tons of flexibility with your brewing endeavors. For example, you could prepare a brew in Summer months to instill it with "Summer" or "Fire" energy. And, you could also use that beverage to mark or honor the southern part of your sacred space! Or, you could prepare a "Fire"-based beverage to use as a libation for Summer rituals. Mix and match however you wish!

For ease of reference, each element and season will be discussed separately in this section:

Spring/Air/East

This is the season of renewal, creativity, transformation, and hope. Traditional ingredients include almond, dandelion, woodruff, anise, honey, clover, daisy, pansy, mint, parsley, sage, and yellow- or pink-colored drinks. For crystal tinctures, turn to mica. To encourage Spring-like energy, prepare these beverages at dawn.

Spring Brews

Whiskey Tea

1 Tbsp. pennyroyal
3 whole cloves
1 cup hot water
1 tsp. mullein

1 tsp. raspberry vinegar
1/2 tsp. lavender
2 tsp. honey

Directions: Steep the pennyroyal, cloves, lavender, and mullein in boiling water for 15 minutes, then strain. To this add honey and mix until fully incorporated, and then add raspberry vinegar. Sip after an asthma attack has begun to fade.

Magickal Associations: Calming winds, Air magick, grounding flights of fancy, the vital breath.

History/Lore: This will also neatly offset allergy and asthma attacks that sometimes come with Spring blossoms.

Flowing Spring

1 gal. apple cider or juice	1 apple tea bag
4 cups real maple syrup	1/4 tsp. orange rind
1 cinnamon stick (optional)	1/3 pkg. yeast

Directions: You can use the basic directions given for wine, except that in this instance, the syrup is your sugar substitute. Open-air fermentation with a towel takes place for 10 days before straining. After this, a loosely covered container will be needed for four to five months until wine is clear. Then bottle with good corks or tightened tops.

Magickal Associations: Renewed life and energy, health and sweet diversions.

History/Lore: In the Spring, tree sap begins to move freely again through the trees, bringing them essential nutrients to bear leaves and come out of their sleep. Cider and apple juice blend nicely with this energy, being strongly associated with well-being.

Butterscotch Breeze

2 1/2 cups milk	2 eggs, beaten frothy
1 pt. butterscotch ice cream	2 tsp. brandy extract
dash nutmeg	

Directions: Place milk and eggs together in blender, mixing until foamy. Next add the remaining ingredients and serve in a mug.

Magickal Associations: New beginnings, renewed health, the energy of Spring and rebirth, the God/dess within.

History/Lore: The symbolism for this beverage comes to us from the ever-versatile egg. The egg has been so important to human foods and trade that literally hundreds of superstitions have evolved around it. The first egg laid by a hen is thought very lucky to the point of encouraging wish-fulfillment, eggs are only to be brought into a house during daylight, and broken eggs have oft been used for scrying forms of divination.

Magickally the egg is considered the sign of fertility, as is seen so readily in Eostre celebrations. Many of the ancient creation stories and deities related to the same have some type of egg figured into them.

Summer/Fire/South

This is the season of energy, purification, and abundance. Traditional ingredients include allspice, basil, beer, all distilled beverages, carrot, celery, chrysanthemum, cinnamon, coffee, daisy, dill, fennel, ginger, garlic, nettle, onion, rose, marigold, nasturtium, bay, clove, nutmeg, orange, radish, tea, wine, and red beverages. For crystal elixirs use amber, carnelian, bloodstone, and lava stone. To encourage Summer-like energy, prepare these beverages at noon.

Summer Brews

Fire Festival

1 tsp. allspice	1 tsp. nutmeg
1/4 tsp. basil	1/2 tsp. peppermint
2 bay leaves	1 tsp. black tea
1/2 tsp. cinnamon	1 whole orange, sliced
6 whole cloves	1 small lime, sliced
1/4 tsp. fennel	2 Tbsp. pomegranate juice
1/2 tsp. ginger	1 cup honey
1 ltr. whiskey	

Directions: Place all your ingredients together in a large container that can be securely sealed. Leave in a sunny window, shaking daily for one month. Do not open during this time. Strain and enjoy hot or cold (hot is probably more magickally appropriate).

Magickal Associations: Vibrant energy, increasing power, the God aspect, mental awareness, the Fire element.

History/Lore: Each of the ingredients for this beverage, including the whiskey as "fire water," are strongly associated with the element of Fire itself. Magickally, Fire is related to the southern portion of the circle and the attributes of vigor, strength, and leadership.

South of the Border

1/2 cup warm tequila
brown sugar to taste
1/4 tsp. nutmeg

1 cup dark roast coffee
cinnamon stick (for stirring)
cream (garnish)

Directions: Mix your tequila, coffee, and sugar together in a personally pleasing balance. Pour into a cup, stirring with a cinnamon stick clockwise, then drizzle cream over top with a sprinkle of nutmeg. Envision the element of Fire filling your inner wells and sparking creativity.

Magickal Associations: Vision, illumination, divination by Fire.

History/Lore: A truly Mexican beverage, this drink is dedicated to the southern quarter of our magick circle, which not only represents the sun, but the devic energy of salamanders—creatures who live and dance in the fires. Thus, this recipe is an excellent libation for fire scrying and the power light has to fill any darkness in your life.

Alternatives: Consider adding other solar flavors to this beverage by way of a slice of orange, a bay leaf, or a sliver of lime.

Fall/Water/West

This is the season focused on the harvest, community, balance, and preparation. Traditional components include apple juice, cardamom, chamomile, mint, thyme, banana, pear, peach, birch (birch beer) catnip, pineapple, berries, cherry juice, chocolate beverages, heather, kiwi, lemon, and mead. For crystal tonics use blue agate, amethyst, fluorite, moonstone, and holy stones. Prepare these beverages at dusk.

Fall Brews

Fall Metheglin

1 cup dried apple	7 bay leaves
2 large cinnamon sticks	1" bruised gingerroot
12 whole cloves	7 whole allspice berries
1 tsp. nutmeg	1 gal. water
3 lbs. dark honey	1/2 pkg. sparkling yeast
1 Tbsp. dried lemon peel	1 Tbsp. dried orange peel
(or fresh from 1 whole fruit)	(or fresh from 1 whole fruit)

Directions: Try to begin this yeast in November of one year so that it will be ready for the next Fall's celebrations. Place all your ingredients except the honey in a two-gallon pan with water. Simmer for one hour so that the water takes on a tea-like quality. Now add the honey, bringing the entire mixture to a boil to skim off scum. Boil for 15 minutes, then follow basic recipe. This mead has a marvelously crisp Fall flavor and is good both hot and cold.

Magickal Associations: The harvest, thankfulness, prudence.

History/Lore: This is basically a mulled beverage that is traditionally made here for enjoyment during Lammas, Fall Equinox, and Thanksgiving into the Yule season. It has all the scents and flavors of the holidays to inspire your magick for this season.

Lammas Libations

1 qt. apple mead	1 tsp. nutmeg
1 tsp. rose water	5 sprigs fresh thyme

Directions: Mix the first three ingredients together and chill. Serve in five glasses with one sprig of thyme each on August 1.

Magickal Associations: Kinship with the fairy kinds or devic realms, psychic vision, and insight. Celebrating the harvest.

History/Lore: Rose, honey, and thyme are all thought to be excellent temptations to the Wee Folk to come for a visit.

And because they are active during Lammas, the first harvest festival, the goal is accentuated by apple mead and a little nutmeg for perception.

Fall Frolic

6 cups hot apple juice	dash nutmeg
2 Tbsp. maple syrup	dash ginger
2 tsp. honey	2 or 3 whole cloves
2 bay leaves	2 or 3 whole allspice
1/2 stick cinnamon	juice of one orange

Directions: Mix syrup and honey with the apple juice until dissolved. Add your spices and allow to infuse like a tea until cool. Strain off whole spices, adding orange juice before freezing. Finish by following the general directions for mead. Possible garnishes include rum sauce, a slice of apple or orange, or a little sweet cream.

Magickal Associations: Any Fall-related festival, the harvest of labors, outcomes, and results.

History/Lore: This is a wonderful, mead-like Autumn beverage, which is also good warm, by the way. It tastes like all the favorite traditional scents of Fall and is especially nice for Thanksgiving gatherings.

Alternative: Peach juice, sacred to many Chinese deities, may be substituted for apple in this recipe for magickal energy toward helping bring wishes into reality.

Winter/Earth/North

A time of rest, frugality, gestation, and grounding. Traditional components include any white beverage, snow or icicles (melted for water), barley, dill, beet juice, any easily stored fruit, cinnamon, honey, coconut, primrose, rhubarb, eggs, and potato. For crystal concoctions use turquoise or moss agate. If possible, prepare these beverages at midnight.

Winter Brews

Earth's Winter Wonder

2 cups coffee, chilled	1 jigger dark rum
3 jiggers coffee liqueur	whipped cream
3 jiggers irish cream liqueur	grated coconut

Directions: Shake your coffee, liqueurs, and rum together in a large container until well blended. Pour this mixture over shaved ice and garnish with whipped cream and coconut. Serves two.

Magickal Associations: Earth healing, Earth magick, rest, as an accent to any Winter festival.

History/Lore: The Earth in this recipe is the rich, dark color like fertile soil. This is neatly hidden by a tuft of snow on top (cream and coconut), the latter of which protects the sleeping land.

Winter Hope

1 cup white grape juice	1 cup pineapple juice
1 cup persimmon juice	2 cups warm ginger ale

Directions: Warm the juices together over a low flame. Add this to the ginger ale, which is at room temperature. Garnish with a fresh flower to remind yourself Spring is not that far away.

History/Lore: Persimmon is the fruit of hope, while the other components of this beverage give it a bright yellow color to remind us of warmer days.

Hot Apple Toddy

1 cup pineapple juice	3 large apples
1/2 lemon	1 orange
dash cinnamon	dash ginger
1 Tbsp. brewers yeast	

Directions: Follow basic recipe for juicing, adding ginger and cinnamon with brewers yeast afterward. Serve warm.

Magickal Associations: Centering, balance.

History/Lore: Apples are associated with spiritual wisdom that can only come through personal insight. The warmth of this drink draws your attention directly to your center of gravity, which can help you to focus energy and bring improved inner harmony.

Leftover Cordial

1 lb. leftover fruit from other brewing efforts

2 cups sugar or honey

1 12-oz. can frozen fruit juice (your choice)

1 ltr. vodka

Directions: Place your leftover fruit and fruit juice (undiluted) in a medium-sized pan to warm. Add sugar or honey and bring to a low boil. Allow this mixture to cool completely, then pour it into a wide mouth jar with vodka. Cover securely and age for three months before straining and serving.

Magickal Associations: Frugality, economy, and conservation of resources.

History/Lore: In a variety of older brewing recipes, I found reference to uses for fruit strainings as part of other wines, meads, and even food items. In this way, our ancestors were wont to waste nothing. For the modern magician, this approach represents a chance to live in greater reciprocity with nature.

FERTILITY AND PROVIDENCE

*"We are not to lead events,
but follow them."*

—Epictetus

The old saying that God helps those who help themselves is not lost on witches. We firmly believe that the more concrete effort we put into our magickal goals, the better the results will be. Nonetheless, there are times in our lives when it seems as if providence needs a boost—when it seems as if life and our options have grown barren. When this happens, it's important to recognize that change must come from both directions. We need to change our perspectives to ones more hopeful and confident, and we need to extend that positive energy out from ourselves to manifest the transformation desired.

With this in mind, the beverages in this section might be best utilized by both drinking and asperging (or libations). This visually and sensually mirrors the within—without equation you're seeking to balance out. Here are some of the traditional components that encourage providence and fertility:

apple juice	banana	cabbage juice
egg	grapes	kiwi
honey	milk	peach juice
strawberry	water	rice milk
grains	alfalfa	raspberries
nuts	dates	figs

Note that when I say fertility that it can apply to far more than getting pregnant. What if you want a fertile garden, or fertile opportunities? Broaden your vision of what various words mean, and you likewise broaden your magickal options!

In terms of timing, I'd suggest preparing these beverages during a waxing or full moon for best results, or during a blue moon if you really need a miracle. For crystal tinctures try amber, coral, or moonstone.

Very Berry

2 qts. elderberries	2 cups brown sugar
2 qts. blackberries	ginger and clove (opt.)
2 qts. water	2 cups brandy

Directions: Place cleaned blackberries and elderberries together in a large pot with water. Simmer over a low flame to extract the juice, crushing and stirring regularly, for 30 minutes. Strain off juice into another pot. Rewarm the liquid so that sugar can be dissolved. Add any personally desired spices at this point and boil for 15 minutes. Cool and add brandy before bottling.

Magickal Associations: Fertility, abundance, a libation for Pan, connection to nature, health, and well-being.

History/Lore: Berries are associated with fertility because of their abundance on bushes. Elderberries and blackberries figure heavily into folk remedies, the tree of the elder itself being boasted as the only wood acceptable for Pan's pipes.

Alternatives: The spices you choose to add to this recipe can aid magickal applications. Nutmeg is one option for luck, or allspice to accentuate the healthful aspects of this beverage.

Men's Mead

1 qt. hickory nut leaves	1/2 qt. black walnut leaves
1 lb. almonds, crushed	1 gal. water
4 lbs. honey	1 lemon
1 orange	1 Tbsp. almond extract
1/2 pkg. of yeast	1/2 qt. oak leaves

Directions: Be sure your leaves are fresh, with no signs of wilting or infestations. Crush them by hand and place in a large pan with almonds. In a separate container, warm water with honey and fruit to a low rolling boil for 20 minutes, skimming. Add extract and follow as with the basic recipe, aging wine for one year.

Magickal Associations: The God aspect and male virility.

History/Lore: The great oak is sacred to Ceres, Zeus, and the Druids of old. The nuts in this recipe represent male sexual organs.

Generative Eggnog

1 doz. eggs, separated	nutmeg (garnish)
1 1/2 cups sugar	1 qt. brandy
1 qt. light cream	dash orange water
2 pints heavy cream, beaten	

Directions: Beat the egg whites until stiff, then set aside. Next, beat egg yokes, slowly adding sugar. Pour this mixture into a large saucepan and heat until very warm, but not boiling. Stir in the brandy, light cream, and orange water, pouring all into the punch bowl. Fold in egg whites, then top with whipped cream and a sprinkling of nutmeg.

Magickal Associations: Generation, inception, creative energy, fertility.

History/Lore: Eggs, being one of the oldest symbols of beginnings and reproduction (some even being credited with the birth of gods) make this the perfect beverage for Eostre and many Spring festivals.

Dried Fruit Tea

6 dried apricots

1/4 cup dried pears

2 fruit tea bags (your choice)

1/2 cup dried apples

4 cups hot water

Directions: While this tea must be prepared hot for proper flavoring to occur, it is delightful served warm or cold. Boil the water to rolling, add the fruit and tea bags. Simmer for 15 minutes, then remove from the heat and strain. Sweeten as desired.

Magickal Associations: Preservation, sustenance, providence, conservation.

History/Lore: Drying of food, perhaps best evidenced by dried meats, has been a traditional means of conserving it for difficult times to many lands and time periods. In the magickal setting, this association can be applied to any situation where you need to provide and sustain specific energy.

Eostre Egg Bowl

12 eggs

2 tsp. vanilla extract

1 tsp. lemon juice

grated lemon peel

nutmeg (garnish)

2 cups sugar

1-2 tsp. brandy extract

1 tsp. orange juice

grated orange peel

Directions: In a double boiler, place your eggs and sugar, beating constantly until fluffy over low flame. Next, add extracts and juices, continuing to beat until warm. To garnish, place a dab of whipped cream on each cup and a sprinkle of lemon, orange, and nutmeg on top.

Magickal Associations: Fecundity, fertility, productivity.

History/Lore: The egg is a traditional symbol of Spring in that even farmers mark the season by when their hens begin laying. Many ancient myths use eggs as part of the creation story.

Bowl of Plenty

1/2 gal. apple cider
1 12-oz. can raspberry juice
cinnamon to taste
ginger to taste
1 cup blueberries
ginger ale (optional)

1 cup whole strawberries
1/2 grapefruit, peeled
1 orange, sliced
1 cup whole cherries
1 thinly sliced lemon

Directions: Mix cider with undiluted raspberry juice and spices. If you prefer, use whole cinnamon and gingerroot so spices can be removed. Stir in fruit slices and chill. Add ginger ale just before serving if desired.

Magickal Associations: Providence, prosperity.

History/Lore: Being representative of the bounty of Earth, this makes an excellent beverage for rituals of thankfulness or during holiday gatherings to bless all in attendance with good fortune.

Couple's Fertility

1 banana
1 cup milk
1 tsp. almond extract

1 peach
2 Tbsp. heavy cream
1 tsp. vanilla extract

Directions: Dice the banana and place it in a blender with milk, flavorings, and a skinned peach cut finely. Mix this until frothy. Meanwhile, using a hand mixer or wire whisk, beat the heavy cream until thick. Pour the juice into a tall glass, one inch at a time, adding a layer of cream until topped off.

History/Lore: In this recipe, I have used the banana to represent the masculine energy, the peach for feminine, the milk for maternity, almond for love, and a little vanilla to aid desire.

Alternatives: At present this drink may be consumed by either sex. You can, however, change the beverage slightly by eliminating the banana for a woman and adding avocado instead. For a man, delete the peach and add a mint leaf.

Prolific Licorice

2 Tbsp. licorice extract	3 cups hot water
2 Tbsp. honey (or to taste)	2 licorice twists (garnish)

Directions: Warm extract, water, and honey together until honey is dissolved. Add more honey or extract to be personally pleasing in taste. Follow general directions for freezing and serving, placing one licorice twist in each glass before filling. Serves two people.

Magickal Association: Providence, especially with regard to essentials.

History/Lore: Bees were always considered messengers of the Gods. When their product, honey, is combined with licorice, which is believed to help relieve hunger, the message sent to the universe is for immediate aid during times of severity.

GROUNDING AND FOUNDATIONS

*"Let us watch well our beginnings,
and results will manage themselves."*

—Alexander Clark

I am an avid fan of Thoreau, who taught us about putting foundations under our "castles in the air." Modern witches agree that this is essential. We cannot lose touch with the real world and our responsibilities therein if our spiritual awakening is to have real meaning. If anything, a good part of magick is centered on being more aware of our surroundings, of others, of the Earth, and of ourselves so that we can manifest the most positive effective changes possible. These beverages are designed to help build that awareness and those foundations.

Additionally, after working magick, many people need to "ground out." If you think of magick like electricity, to keep from getting shocked, it's wise to have proper grounding. Similarly, magick carries a lot of energy that can leave a person spaced out and a little disconnected. Grounding beverages help bring you back to earth and refocus your mind on the here-and-now.

Some of the components used in grounding are exactly what you might expect: root vegetables because of the symbolic value inherent in having a deep connection to the earth. Here are some others:

beans	carrots	potatoes
eggs	grains	turnips
garlic	basil	seeds

For timing, I'd suggest preparing these beverages during the daytime to accentuate the role of the conscious, logical mind. Make or serve this beverage from a squared off container (a symbol of the Earth) or one that's black like soil. For a crystal tonic use obsidian.

Completion Cordial

1 qt. distilled beverage (your choice)
1/2 Tbsp. sesame seed
1/2 Tbsp. caraway seed
1/2 Tbsp. fennel seed
3/4 cup sugar

1/2 Tbsp. cumin seed
1/2 Tbsp. aniseed
1/2 Tbsp. angelica seed
1/2 Tbsp. coriander seed
1/4 cup hot water

Directions: Place your seeds together in a blender, food processor, or mortar to grind them into a fine powder. Put these in a large covered container with your chosen beverage. This needs to age for 30 days.

After aging, take the sugar and dissolve in hot water. Carefully strain your seeded liquid into a different bottle, adding the sugar mix. Shake well until incorporated. Rebottle and age for another month before consuming.

Magickal Associations: Thoroughness, finishing projects, celebrating variety.

History/Lore: The number seven (the number of seeds used for this cordial) is one of completion. There are seven days in the week, seven wonders in the world, and in the biblical account of creation, it took seven days to form the Earth. Seven is also a potent number for moon magicks and improved insight.

Alternatives: Vodka is a good choice for use as the distilled beverage in this recipe; it has a neutral flavor that integrates the herbs well. Any seed herb (like dill) can be substitute into this recipe for another seed that you may not enjoy or just for variety. Likewise, try changing the number of seeds to reflect different magickal goals, such as five seeds for versatility and awareness. Note: This may also be used for fertility for men (seed representing the sperm).

Build from the Bottom Up!

1 pt. grenadine	1 Tbsp. orange juice
1 pt. triple sec	2 Tbsp. sugar
1 pt. creme de menthe	2 pts. heavy cream

Directions: Pour the grenadine into a small punch bowl. If you like, add some fruit in this layer (like cherries). Next, very slowly pour the triple sec on top of the grenadine by touching the bottle to the rim, and letting it seep down the side of the bowl. Follow this procedure again with the creme de menthe, succeeded by one pint of the heavy cream. Next, beat the remaining pint of cream until thick and frothy, adding juice and sugar. Float this *carefully* on top of the whole. The end result looks much like a layered mountain with snow at the peak!

Magickal Associations: Fashioning foundations in the best possible way for long-lasting results.

History/Lore: It has been an adventurous pastime of many bartenders to learn techniques of layering liqueurs. This particular punch bowl only looks pretty until you serve out of it, when the layers get blended.

The Recipes

Wishes Are Brewing

1/2 cup heavy cream	4 cups water
1 tsp. vanilla extract	2 Tbsp. dark roast coffee
1 egg white	1 tsp. ground dandelion root
1 Tbsp. sugar	1/2 tsp. ginseng

Directions: Mix your coffee with finely ground dandelion root and the ginseng, then place in pot to brew with water. While this drips, beat your heavy cream and egg white on high until peaks begin to form. Add extract and sugar at this time, placing a hefty portion into each serving cup. Pour the coffee into the cup by slowly letting it slip down the sides. This allows some cream to mix in and the rest to remain on top like mountain peeks.

Magickal Associations: Putting foundations under goals and aspirations; hope and fancy.

History/Lore: Ginseng roots, besides being regarded as a tonic, were sometimes carved or tossed into running water to help bring wishes into reality. Dandelion is similarly regarded, its ground roots often acting as a coffee substitute.

Slavic Bread Wine

1/2 lb. dark rye bread	1/2 lb. buckwheat meal
2 large apples	1 gal. water
1/2 cup raisins	3 Tbsp. dry active yeast
2 cups brown sugar	1/2 cup mincemeat

Directions: Slice and toast rye bread, then set aside. Meanwhile, boil the water in a large pot with apples that have been peeled and diced, for 30 minutes. Remove this from the heat, adding toasted rye pieces and barley that need to soak for four hours. Strain thoroughly. Dissolve yeast in warm water, adding this to the juice along with minced meat. Follow as with basic recipe, pouring into a gallon jug with raisins and setting in a cool area to ferment for one week. Strain again and chill for use.

Magickal Associations: Grounding out excess energy. Good wishes, comfort of hearth and home, lifting burdens.

History/Lore: Known by the local name of kvass, this wine's title literally translates to mean "leaven." Because kvass is only mildly alcoholic, it was often part of the meal table and considered quite healthy.

Earth Beer

6 apples, baked till soft   1/2 cup brown sugar
1 tsp. nutmeg   1 tsp. ginger
5 cups hot non-alcoholic beer or apple wine

Directions: Peel the apples, mashing the fruit with brown sugar and spices (more sweetening may be added, if desired). Mix this with ale or wine and enjoy as a liquid dessert!

Magickal Associations: Earth magick, wisdom, ecology. Connecting with the Earth element.

History/Lore: In certain parts of Europe, a version of this drink was often served on August 1 (Lammas Tide) to honor the spiritual protector who presides over fruit, seeds, and Earth's bounty. Not surprisingly, Lammas was sometimes referred to as "the day of the apple fruit."

Turtle Tenacity

1 pt. butter-toffee ice cream   1 1/2 cups milk
1 Tbsp. hot fudge sauce   1 Tbsp. hot caramel sauce
nuts (garnish)

Directions: The ability to create a strong foundation is usually a function of the conscious mind, so allow the ice cream to get soft in the light of the sun. Pour this into a blender with the milk and sauce on medium speed, beating until frothy. Garnish with nuts of your choice.

Magickal Associations: Structure, boldness, assertive speech, self-assurance, building confidence.

History/Lore: While I am playing on a pun for a popular candy here, the symbolism of the turtle is no less important to this beverage. Visualize yourself like a great sea tortoise, slowly but powerfully emerging from your shell while drinking.

Baked Potato Pie

2 baked potatoes, peeled   1 large onion
2 scallions with tops   2 cloves garlic
1 cup skim milk   salt and pepper to taste

Directions: Once your potatoes are baked and peeled, you can follow the basic recipe for juicing. This is best enjoyed without straining and has a consistency like mashed potatoes or cream of potato soup.

Magickal Associations: Establishing healthy beginnings and strong foundations; Earth magick.

History/Lore: Potatoes, being a root plant, help us connect more directly with Gaia energies. Carry one with you into circle when working Earth Magick and hold it in your palms as a focus.

Financial Foundations

1 cup currants, juiced   1 cup cherries, juiced
1 cup blackberries, juiced   1 Tbsp. honey
1 orange, juiced   1 bundle of grapes
2 cups apple juice

Directions: Place all ingredients after juice extraction into a blender and mix at high speed until bubbly. Leave in a glass with the grapes hinged on the side.

History/Lore: Most of the fruits chosen for this drink are connected with building financial security; however, the energy can be put towards other areas of your life where some opulence is needed, like creativity.

Security's Simmering

1/2 cup plain yogurt   1 tsp sugar
1/2 cup chocolate milk   1 tsp. mint extract

Directions: This is a wonderful beverage that tastes akin to the Girl Scout thin mints. Place the first four ingredients in a blender (or use a hand beater) to mix thoroughly. Garnish with a Girl Scout cookie of your choice.

Magickal Associations: Resilience, stability, security. Energy for good deeds.

History/Lore: Minthe was once a nymph changed into this indestructible ground plant by Persephone. Mint is sacred to Aphrodite, and it is also considered a good herb for protection and prosperity.

HAPPINESS

"It's a wine of virtuous powers,
my mother made it out of wildflowers."

—Samuel T. Coleridge

Next to good health, happiness is among the qualities that many people seek to fill out the corners of their lives. Witches are no different. We want a joyful existence. It is certainly not selfish to use our magick as a means of attracting and manifesting that joy. Why not? Because a happy person is also one much more able to give of themselves. And, actually, happiness tends to be very contagious!

Some of the traditional components that promote cheer and delight include:

basil	blue juices	bubbly liquids
catnip	chocolate	daisy
dandelion	marjoram	mint
orange	rose	thyme
vanilla	wine	lavender
berries	apple	cherry
honey	apricot	lemon
cloves		

In terms of timing these beverages, don't work on cloudy or gray days. Joy is sunny in its disposition—no dark clouds allowed! Think in terms of brightly colored juices that are as light and radiant as you wish your mood to be! As for crystal tinctures, turn to cat's eye and gold.

Joyful Ale

1 lb. sweet cherries　　　4 cups sugar
10 whole cloves　　　　　3 qts. strong ale

Directions: Prick cherries with a toothpick on all sides, then place them in a gallon container with a lid. An excellent choice is a container made of wood or earthenware. Sprinkle the sugar over top of these, then fill with the ale. Cover loosely as fermentation should begin within 48 hours. When the rapid bubbling has ceased, strain, cork, and store for six months to a year before drinking. The remaining cherries make marvelous pies and conserves.

Magickal Associations: Clear vision, unhindered joys.

History/Lore: Cloves appeared in Europe between 4 and 6 C.E There, they remained mostly a culinary herb, but modern magickal practitioners often view them as protective, cleansing, and an aid to psychic sight. Cherries always engender thoughts of clear Spring days and happy children playing outside.

Alternatives: One very tasty alternative is strawberries mixed with a stout beer to strengthen love.

Pineapple Pleasure

1/2 gal. water　　　　　3 16-oz. jars pineapple chunks
1 orange　　　　　　　　(in juice)
4 lbs. honey (orange blossom)　1/2 gal. pineapple juice
1/2 pkg. of yeast

Directions: Place pineapple chunks (juice and all) in a large pan with the water, sliced orange, and honey. Bring to a low rolling boil for 30 to 40 minutes, skimming any residue off the top, then add pineapple juice reducing heat to a simmer for 10 more minutes. Cool, then follow directions for yeast and bottling given in basic recipe. Aging time after final corking is about six to eight months for a sweet wine; one year for dry.

Magickal Associations: Happy celebrations, hospitality, joyful meetings or discoveries.

History/Lore: As a fruit native to tropical Americas, the pineapple was unknown until the New World was discovered, going by the native name "nana," which translates to mean "fragrance." Slowly images of the pineapple worked themselves into all manner of American furniture, architecture, etc. as an emblem of pleasant welcome.

Wine and Song

1/2 qt. strawberries hulled	1 cup sugar
3 sliced peaches	1/2 gal. sangria
2 cups fresh diced pineapple	1 bottle champagne

Directions: Put both the fruit and sugar in a large bowl, stirring to cover the fruit well. Crush half of the fruit while you blend, then let this sit for one hour to produce juice. Next, add the sangria and champagne (both chilled), adding ice just before serving. Makes just under one gallon.

Magickal Associations: Joyful celebrations, cessation of cares and worries, positive exchange between new companions.

History/Lore: In the late 1600s, when sailing voyage was popular, some sailors who landed in India got quite a surprise. They were greeted with a fruity liquid mixed with spirits that was very refreshing. The potency, however, was deceptive and the crew quickly found themselves intoxicated and quite giddy to the point of spontaneous song.

Vostorg

1 cup cognac	2 Tbsp. cherry liquor
1 tsp. lemon juice	2 cherries (garnish)
3 or 4 ice cubes	

Directions: Depending on personal preference, this cordial can be prepared one of two ways. First is to place all the ingredients except cherries in a blender for a whipped, icy beverage topped with whole cherries. Second is to simply place the components in a shaker and serve over ice.

Magickal Associations: One-world perspectives, pleasure, happiness, broadening outlooks.

History/Lore: Coming to us from Russia, this beverage's name translates as meaning "delight."

Alternatives: One especially nice touch with this drink is to add a fresh, white gardenia as garnish to encourage peace.

Beneficent Balm Blend

1 1/2 qt. balm leaves	2 gal. water
1 1/2 qts. elderberries, pressed	4 1/2 lbs. sugar
1 1/2 qts. raspberries, pressed	1 pkg. wine yeast

Directions: Place the herbs and fruit in the water in a large pan over medium heat. Press the berries regularly to extract as much juice as possible. After about 30 minutes, add sugar, stirring until dissolved. Continue cooking for another half hour. Turn off heat and cool to lukewarm. Strain well. In a small container, mix yeast with a half cup of warm water, stirring once. Let sit for 15 minutes, then add to lukewarm fruit juice. Cover the pan with a towel for 24 hours, then strain again into a loosely covered container. Watch the wine for signs that fermentation is finishing (namely a decrease in bubbles). Strain once more, then bottle and rack. Age eight months.

Magickal Associations: Lifting heavy spirits, amiableness, cheerful countenance.

History/Lore: Arabic tales suggest that balm has the remarkable ability to make an individual more agreeable and easier to love. Beyond this, it was a favored herb for fevers, headache, and cooking, its minty-lemon scent generally improving sad spirits. Elder is mentioned in medicinal texts as early as Egypt, most poplar at the turn of the century for throat infections. Raspberry brings a soothing effect to blend the lot together.

Happiness Wine

3 qts. strawberries

3 large seedless oranges

3 lbs. sugar

1/4" gingerroot

1 gal. water

1/3 pkg. yeast

Directions: Hull strawberries and peel all but one of the oranges. Slice the strawberries and oranges into your brew pot, then follow basic recipe. Extra straining may be required.

Magickal Associations: Revitalization, health, happiness.

History/Lore: In the East, the orange is an emblem of satisfaction and pleasure.

Black Currant Cheer

1 qt. raspberry juice

sugar to taste

1/3 lb. budding black currant

shoots

Directions: Warm raspberry juice over low flame, allowing currant buds to simmer for about 20 minutes. Remove from heat and cool. Strain, tasting for personally desired sweetness, then enjoy!

Magickal Associations: Joy, relief from depression, sympathy, charity.

History/Lore: Currants get their name from Corinth, Greece, where they were first discovered. In the language of flowers they mean, "your frown will kill me." Raspberry branches have been regarded as protective (due to thorns), while the fruit itself is one of happiness.

Celebration Jubilation

1 qt. ginger ale

1 qt. soda water

1 qt. white grape juice

2 cups apricot juice

2 cups sugar

1 cup lemon juice

1 cup raspberries

borage flowers

Directions: Mix together your sodas and juices, slowly adding sugar until the taste is pleasing. Float whole raspberries on top of the punch and chill. Place borage around the edge of the punch bowl before serving.

Magickal Associations: Jubilee, merry-making, glad tidings.

History/Lore: Sparkling waters have long been used in various forms of celebration and were even considered lucky. Raspberry is added for pleasure and borage flowers for joy.

Coffee Contentment

6 eggs	grated lemon peel
1/2 cup sugar	3 cups strong fruity coffee
1/2 cup apple juice	1 Tbsp. brandy flavoring

Directions: Beat eggs until frothy, then slowly add grated peel from one lemon and sugar until thick. Set aside while you mix together the remaining ingredients. Fold this into the egg mixture very slowly. Serve in chilled glasses.

Magickal Associations: Joyful gatherings, sojourns to see friends and family.

History/Lore: A version of this recipe is often served at Yule festivities in Denmark.

Alternatives: For abundantly happy energy, choose a raspberry coffee base and use strawberry syrup in place of sugar to taste.

HEALTH

*"Good health and good sense
are two of life's greatest blessings"*

—Publilius Syrus

Folk remedials used beverages as their base for thousands of years. For proof we need look no further than the Roman battlefield, the Celtic hearth, and Greek curatives. In these locations and many more, physicians used liqueurs laced with herbs to ease the pain of wounds, and nearly every other imaginable illness. In Greek writings, specifically those of Athenaeus, we find a cure for hangovers that consists of cabbage water and a good nap, while Proverbs tells us that we should "give strong drink to him that is ready to perish and wine to those that be of heavy hearts (31:4)!"

Many of these beverage recipes were called physics or simples, the latter name coming from the simple, yet time-honored nature of the cure. A goodly number of the recipes included magickal methods in the instructions, including what day of the week to harvest the herbs and when to prepare and administer the prescription! So while the ancient healers were depending on a sound body of herbal knowledge to cure, they also remembered that patients were spiritual beings too—and that the spirit needed tending as much as the body.

This is a very good lesson for modern Witches to remember in their own healing beverages. We should look to accredited herbalists advice on what best to include, but not overlook common sense, medical knowledge, and our spiritual self for assistance either.

Bear in mind as you read these recipes that specific conditions (like a cold or flu) will have specific herbs that have been shown effective against them. So the list that follows only includes the ingredients that are magickally active for promoting health and wellness:

almond	apple	ginger
lavender	lettuce	marjoram
mead	milk	nutmeg
rosemary	Sage	Water
wine	green juices	

In terms of timing you have some flexibility here. A beverage aimed at maintaining health might be best made during the waxing moon, whereas one aimed at banishing an existing problem would be made during the waning moon. For crystal tonics turn to agate, carnelian, holy stones, and quartz.

Spice-Away Sickness

1 cup dried french lavender	1" minced gingerroot
1 - 1" cinnamon stick	4 whole allspice berries
4 whole cloves	1 tsp. nutmeg
1 qt. water	pinch sage
1 qt. brandy	1 cup raisins
2 cups honey	2 Tbsp. rose water

Directions: All dry ingredients except the raisins should be ground finely, then put into a large container with honey, raisins, and rose water. The brandy is then poured over the entire mixture. Cover this container well, and allow it to sit in the sun (or a warm area) for 20 days, shaking regularly. Strain thoroughly, rebottling the clear fluid for use. Store in cool, dark area.

Magickal Associations: Strength, vitality, recuperative powers, the spirit of life.

History/Lore: This recipe is a version of a Medieval Aqua Vitae that knights often drank before battle. It was also frequently given to those presumed to be dead, with the belief that such a potent combination of healthful herbs might restore breath and vitality.

Wellness Blend

9 cored apples (small)	dash nutmeg
1 cup packed brown sugar	12 whole cloves
1 1/2 qts. dark ale	3 eggs separated
1/2" gingerroot, sliced	

Directions: Roll the apples in the brown sugar. Place these in a 375-degree oven for 40 minutes. Meanwhile, warm the ale with ginger and other spices. Separately, beat egg whites and egg yolks until thickened, then fold them together, slowly pouring this mixture into the ale, beating with a wire whisk quickly as you go. Makes enough for six to eight people.

Magickal Associations: Health, well-being, good wishes, and fruitfulness.

History/Lore: A version of the Anglo-Saxon treat, Wassail, which literally translates to "be well," this beverage found itself consumed throughout the Yule season.

Sniffle Stopper

1/2 cup whiskey	dash ginger
1/2 cup warm water	1 to 2 Tbsp. honey
2 to 3 eucalyptus leaves	1 Tbs. fresh lemon juice
1 Tbsp. fresh orange juice	

Directions: Heat the water until almost boiling with the eucalyptus leaves in it. Remove the leaves, then add all remaining ingredients, drinking before bedtime. The remedial value of this beverage can be accentuated magickally by working during a waning moon, so the sickness will likewise shrink.

Magickal Associations Return to health and well-being (more on the physical level than emotional or spiritual).

History/Lore: This recipe comes from my own "backyard," so to speak, where I have tried to combine the best herbal decongestant with other healthful fruits for best results. I have found this drink helps improve sleep and breathing during cold and flu season.

Spicy Orange Fitness

1 qt. mulled mead	2 qts. orange picot tea
1 cup orange juice	1 sliced lemon
1 sliced orange	1/2 cup honey (to taste)
6 pieces cinnamon stick	6 whole cloves

Directions: Make your tea and pour it hot into a large container with the cinnamon stick pieces (one inch each is good), cloves, and honey. Likewise warm the mead and orange juice together, and add this to the tea blend mixing thoroughly. Serve hot with a slice of orange and lemon in each cup.

Magickal Associations: Health and well-being, vitality, return of physical balance.

History/Lore: The Portuguese believe that the original orange tree transplanted from China to Europe, and which birthed all other orange bearing trees, still lives quite heartily today in Lisbon.

Alternatives: Try an apple-spice tea with apple juice in this recipe in place of the orange for similar and very tasty magickal results.

Cold Tonic

1/2 gal. boiling water	10 eucalyptus leaves
1/2 tsp. sage	1/2 tsp. rosemary
1/2 tsp. anise	1/2 tsp. thyme
1/2 tsp. valerian	1/2 tsp. comfrey
1/2 tsp. gingerroot, bruised	1/2 tsp. yarrow buds
1 tsp. chamomile	5 to 10 fresh mint leaves
lemon rind	orange rind
1 bay leaf	

Directions: This mixture is best steeped for one hour then strained. Stir counterclockwise to banish illness. I do not recommend drinking it cold as the eucalyptus is far more effective warm.

Magickal Associations: Easing rough nerves, rest, cleansing, amulet creation, prophecy, calm understanding.

History/Lore: Tried and true from my own household, this keeps well in an airtight jar in the refrigerator and also eases asthma. Magickally, bay leaves were sometimes used to write spells on and were often employed in the preparation of amulets.

Elixir of Health

1 cup pineapple juice	watercress (optional)
1/2 cup cucumber peeled and seeded	crushed ice
	1 sprig parsley

Directions: Use general directions given for juicing.

Magickal Associations: General well-being, physical fitness, and protection of one's vitality.

History/Lore: Because of its spiny exterior and cutting flavor, pineapple is regarded as a shielding fruit. Cucumber peels have long been recommended by folk healers to relieve headaches, and the decorative sprig of parsley on our plates dates back to Roman superstition about it keeping the food safe from contamination.

Hale and Hardy Cider

Directions: Cider is unique among fermented beverages in that it contains one ingredient... in this case, apples. Depending on the type you choose, the amount of cider you have once finished will vary. The best ciders are made from a variety of apples, rich in juice, including Macintosh, Delicious, Granny Smith, and Crab apples.

To prepare, clean and chop your fruit, putting it through a juicer, blender, or even a food grinder to release the internal juices. Then you will need to strain several times, pressing with the back of a wooden spoon to express as much liquid as possible from your chosen batch of apples.

Once you have it as clear as possible, place in a glass jar or wooden barrel tightly stopped. Check this twice a week (kept in a cool area) for signs of fermentation. Once it has reached a personally pleasing level of natural carbonation, turn the liquid to a large pot on the stove and warm to just under the boiling point. Cool and store. The cider in this form can be kept longer without risk of turning to vinegar. It may also be spiced and served hot or cold.

Magickal Associations: Continual good health and wisdom; refreshment, rejuvenation.

History/Lore: While we have all heard the saying about an apple a day, the best season to drink hard cider for well-being has always been regarded as the harvest. This is probably attributable to the abundance of the fruit during that season. Warmed with spices, this is thought to be a good restorative for energy and a way to ease fevers.

Emotional Healing Brew

1 pot extra strong coffee
1 whole orange, seeded
1 cup orange juice
1 cup slivered almonds

whipped cream
whole almonds
3/4 to 1 cup sugar syrup

Directions: Blend together your hot coffee, orange, and juice with sugar until frothy. Freeze as per directions for frappes. When flaking with the fork, mix in slivered almonds. Garnish with almond- or orange-flavored whipped cream and two whole nuts.

Magickal Associations: Energy for healing relationships of any nature and emotional wounds.

History/Lore: Almonds have been used readily in early medicine for insomnia and headaches. Oranges are a love fruit, their blossoms often being carried by brides at ancient weddings. Coffee adds active energy to this beverage-spell.

Sweet Health

1 cup orange juice
1 tsp. vanilla
1 slice of orange (garnish)

1 Tbsp. rosemary
2 Tbsp. whipped cream

Directions: Make a warm tea of the orange juice, rosemary, and vanilla, then strain. Serve slightly warm with one tablespoon of whipped cream blended in and one on top for garnish with a slice of fresh orange.

History/Lore: While many people think of rosemary only in terms of remembrance, in the Middle Ages it was lauded as having many restorative qualities for health. The high content of vitamin C in oranges aids this feature.

INSPIRATION AND CREATIVITY

"Poets are the hierophants of an unapprehended inspiration;
the mirrors of the gigantic shadows
which futurity casts upon the present."

—Percy Shelley

Magick has a kind of poetry to it, in the way it goes together, in the invocations and spells. And modern Witches are the poets who use inspiration, creativity, and imagination to create new forms of magick suited to our ever-changing world. If the metaphysical arts become stagnant, the positive energy they can create dies. By its very definition magick is to change, and therefore we must use a little creativity to keep up with that transformation process.

But what happens when you go to inspiration's well and find it wanting? You've scanned dozens of books, talked to various people, and just can't seem to find something that motivates invention. That's when you need to quaff a few beverages that can provide the internal nudge you're lacking.

Some of the ingredients recommended for creativity are:

allspice	honey	mead
water	yellow beverages	wine
almond	dandelion	lavender
maple flavoring	mint	sage
pomegranate juice		

Make these when the moon is full, and drink them from a silver-toned cup. For crystal tinctures use green or clear quartz.

Death by Chocolate

1 scoop chocolate fudge ice cream	1 cup chocolate yogurt
	1/4 cup chocolate chips
1 cup chocolate milk	swirl chocolate syrup (garnish)

Directions: Place all ingredients except syrup into a blender on low speed for about 2 to 3 minutes. Add more milk if it is too thick. Beat on medium for another two minutes. Pour into a large glass, swirling a little chocolate syrup on top. Sit down and pat yourself on the back for just being a unique person, and enjoy!

Magickal Associations: Inspiration when it's lacking. Self-love and pampering, sweet things in life, simple luxuries.

History/Lore: There is very strong scientific evidence to suggest that chocoholics actually do receive a kind of unique pleasure and motivation from eating this substance.

Inventive Petals

1 qt. warm apple wine
  or hard cider
2 oz. sugar or honey
stick cinnamon
1 lemon, sliced

1/2 cup woodruff flowers
  freshly picked
1/4 pt. water
1 orange, sliced

Directions: Allow the woodruff to set in room-temperature wine or cider for a half hour, then remove. To this add sugar and water. Pour into punch bowl, garnishing with sliced fruit and cinnamon stick. May be served hot, if desired.

Magickal Associations: Woodruff as a traditional May flower brings with it the refreshing inspiration of Spring, especially for new projects. Apple adds wisdom to that creative spark.

History/Lore: Germans call this lovely white blossom the master of the woods. Its white petals are considered sacred to the Goddess. Magickally, woodruff is used to protect against negative energies that could cause creative blockage.

One for the Noggin'

5 egg yolks
8 Tbsp. sugar
1 1/2 tsp. vanilla extract
2 drops yellow food color

1 qt. milk
1 1/2 cups cognac
nutmeg

Directions: Beat egg yokes with sugar until well incorporated. Next, add the vanilla with the milk, which has been heated to very hot. Stir in cognac, food color, and a dash of nutmeg, and then pour into the punch bowl. If possible, serve in yellow cups.

Magickal Associations: Creativity, imagination.

History/Lore: This version of eggnog was popular in the 17th century throughout France. It is a wonderful golden color, bringing a little solar warmth to any Winter celebration.

Enlivening Fires

2 large tomatoes
2 red peppers
1 tsp. lime juice
rosemary (garnish)

2 cloves garlic
1 cup chopped red cabbage
1 tsp. hot sauce

Directions: Follow the directions given for juicing. Please note, however, that hot sauce may be increased or decreased according to your tolerance. A fresh sprig of rosemary is placed in each glass.

Magickal Association: Creative motivation (putting a fire under a project); Fire magick, drastic change, the energy of the Phoenix, purification.

History/Lore: The traditional herbs, plants, and colors of Fire combine in this drink to quite literally spark your creative source from inside out! An appropriate beverage for Beltane and many Summer observances.

Winds of Inspiration

4 lemons, juiced
1 tsp. vanilla
2 scoops of lemon sherbet
1 cup heavy cream

1 egg
2 bananas, mashed
1 star fruit, sliced
3/4 cup sugar syrup

Directions: Place lemon juice, vanilla, and sherbet in a pan to warm. Meanwhile, beat cream until fluffy. Slowly mix this with the warm liquid, adding your sugar and a beaten egg. Freeze at this point, moving the frozen crushed beverage to the blender with the bananas. Pour from the blender into glasses decorated with star fruit. Serves two.

Magickal Associations: Divination, prophesy, creativity, and any Air-related magick.

History/Lore: Yellow is associated with the energy of Inventiveness and the Air element allowing our dreams to take flight. Additionally bananas are for fertility of efforts and lemon for clarity in goals. The star fruit is a wonderful addition here, already bearing the shape of the magickal pentagram.

Pomegranate Notions

2 cups pomegranate seeds, juiced
dash cinnamon

1 cup ginger ale or soda
dash ginger
1 lemon balm leaf (garnish)

Directions: Juice the pomegranate seeds by placing them in a bowl and pressing with the back of a spoon. Strain this off, adding it to your ginger ale with the spices sprinkled on top and the leaf hinged on the edge of your serving glass.

History/Lore: Pomegranate encourages fertile ideas, while both ginger and cinnamon add energy for achievement. The carbonated soda is for effervescence!

KINSHIP, UNITY, FRIENDSHIP

*"While wine and friendship crown the board,
we'll sing the joys they both afford"*

—John Dryden

There is little in life that does not benefit from having good friends, a harmonious home, and unified groups. We deal so much with group dynamics these days—at the office, in our covens, and even in our families—that having magickal methods to help keep these settings tranquil is a great blessing. Beverages are certainly one means to that end.

A Witch's Beverages and Brews

Consider for a moment the symbolism of a single cup shared among people and the trust it implies. This symbolism is very ancient and has appeared in many different cultural settings, so it gives us pause to understand that the unity is, in part, an act of acceptance. When we drink from the cup, we accept the energy of the beverage into ourselves, and we accept the gesture offered from another. Please keep this in mind when you prepare and drink the beverages in this chapter.

Some of the ingredients noted for kinship, friendship, and unity include:

lemon	yellow beverages	rose
wine	passion fruit	basil
lilac	gardenia (garnish)	almond
anise	plum	balm
clove	cinnamon	

The timing for these beverages depends a lot on your perspectives. I feel that both solar and lunar energies would benefit them because one helps us think clearly, and the other helps us feel. Trust your instincts. For crystal elixirs, turn to geodes and loadstone.

Plum Unity

1 qt. brandy or vodka	1 lb. ripe plums
2 cups sugar	

Directions: Place all your ingredients together in a large crock, well sealed. Shake daily for eight weeks. Strain the liquid off into bottles, which should be sealed and aged six months before consumption. The fruit may be used for tarts, pies, or a spiked dessert with cream garnish after straining.

Magickal Associations: Safety and open discourse among family and friends; kinship.

History/Lore: This cordial comes to us from the Ukraine, where it is a favored beverage on cold nights with family or friends. Bits of the plum tree were sometimes used as protection to rural homes, by hanging the branches on the entryway so no avarice could come between those within.

Melodious Mint

1 qt. packed balm leaves	1 qt. packed mint leaves
8 cloves	1" piece vanilla bean
(the number of completion)	2 lbs. dark honey
1 gal. water	1/2 pkg. yeast

Directions: In one pan crush the balm and mint leaves. In another, bring the water to a boil and pour over top the herbs. Let this mixture stand for one day, then strain, squeezing excess juice from the leaves. Place this liquid over a low flame, adding vanilla bean and honey. Stir until the honey is dissolved, continuing to warm for about 30 minutes, skimming any residue from the top. Cool the liquid to lukewarm, and then follow the remainder of directions from the basic recipe.

Magickal Associations: Friendship, happiness, amicable feelings.

History/Lore: Mint is the herb of wisdom, being considered helpful in improving spirits. The Israelites were known to cover the floors of their temples and homes with mint leaves to welcome and refresh honored guests. Balm is very compatible to this energy, helping to make people more agreeable and joyous.

Persians used cloves to rekindle the fires of a relationship gone cold, often mixed with rose water and a bit of prayer from the Koran. The potent flavor and scent of the clove has also given it associations with energy for protection, perhaps best directed towards relationships.

Warm Up to Someone

1 gal. water	3 lbs. clover honey
3 oz. fresh gingerroot, bruised	2 lemons
1 orange	1 cup raisins
1/2 pkg. yeast	2 large cinnamon sticks (broken)

Directions: Dissolve the honey in warm water, adding the gingerroot (cut up), cinnamon, and raisins. Bring this to a boil for one hour, then strain liquid into a separate container. Peel the lemons and orange, squeezing their juice into the container with the gingered water and add the rinds. Dissolve the yeast in warm water then add, stirring well. Follow as per basic recipe, allowing mead to age eight months to a year before use.

Magickal Associations: Sympathy, cordial feelings, affection, health.

History/Lore: This is similar to an Irish beverage that adds nutmeg and spirits to the recipe, called Usquebaugh, and is used to warm chilled bones.

Sympathetic Sangria

2 pts. strong tea	4 whole cloves
4 Tbsp. orange juice	1 slice lemon rind
4 Tbsp. sugar	1 pt. sangria
1 stick cinnamon	1 sliced orange

Directions: Heat your ingredients together, except for the orange slices. Once warmed to a tea-like consistency, pour into a punch bowl and garnish with oranges. Or, you may chill first, and then serve cold.

Magickal Associations: Kinship, leisurely pursuits, and friendly conversation.

History/Lore: Both wine and tea have a cordial, comfortable appeal, making this a very relaxing beverage perfect for quiet afternoons with friends. This drink has the additional benefit of clearing the throat during allergy season.

Fruity Kinship

2 qts. fresh strawberries	8 cups sugar
4 pink grapefruit (large)	1 slice lemon
1 lb. seedless raisins	1/3 pkg. wine yeast
1 black tea bag	

Directions: Juice your grapefruit, extracting as much liquid as possible. Place this in a large container with raisins and water, and then leave overnight in a warm area. Move this kettle to the stove, adding strawberries, the tea bag, sugar, and lemon. Follow basic cooking recipe for wine except that you should allow cloth-covered fermentation for six days before straining off berries and raisins. This will allow a fuller-flavored wine.

After first fermentation, wine should be allowed to set for four months before another straining, then aged an additional six months before serving.

Magickal Associations: Kinship, leisure, and positive attitudes.

History/Lore: While strawberries are a traditional love fruit, the light pink coloration of this wine turns its energy more towards matters of friendship and simple pleasures.

Herbal Harmony

1/4 cup french lavender dried	3 leaves fresh mint
3 to 4 allspice beads	1/4 tsp. thyme
1/4 tsp. angelica root	1/2 lemon rind
1/4 tsp. sage	1 gal. basic recipe

Directions: Follow the basic recipe, adding herbs after the boiling process to create a tea. Lemon rind may require the use of additional sweetener.

Magickal Associations: Accord, agreement, unity.

History/Lore: Lavender and mint are employed here to promote happiness and harmony. The next two components are for healing. Angelica will aid in dispersing negativity, lemon to building friendships, and sage is for wisdom.

Alternative: Where a tremendous amount of discernment is required, add a cup of freshly diced peaches to the mixture. If this is going to be consumed in a group setting, I suggest adding one allspice bead or mint leaf to represent each person to the pot. This way, their desire to become unified is literally cooked right into the brew! In this case, lavender can be regarded as an optional ingredient.

Loving Cup

4 cups apple cider
2 cinnamon sticks
1/2 cup blanched almonds

4 whole cloves
1 cup raisins
sugar or honey

Directions: Warm the cider over low flame with other ingredients incorporated. Once sugar or honey is dissolved, this is ready to serve. If desired, the beverage may be chilled or even enjoyed as a frappe. You can leave spices in or strain, depending on what is most personally pleasing.

Magickal Associations: Warm feelings, kinship, and the love of friends.

History/Lore: A favorite Swedish drink during Winter celebrations, this glogg may be enjoyed hot or cold. For a special treat, roll the almonds after cooking in a bit of honey and offer them to someone special to spark some romance.

Tea Wine

20 Earl Grey tea bags
1 orange sliced
1/2" gingerroot bruised
1/3 pkg. yeast

1 tsp. lemon juice
2 lbs. sugar
1 gal. water

Directions: Steep the tea bags in the boiled water overnight. Remove and press any liquid out that you can. Place this container back on the stove, adding the remaining ingredients except yeast. Remove citrus fruit once the tea is cooled to lukewarm, and then follow basic recipe for wine. This yields a dry wine that has a flavor similar to sun tea.

Magickal Associations: Friendly conversation, relaxation, social gatherings.

History/Lore: One legend has it that the Emperor She Nudge (also known as a great healer) invented hot tea when some nearby leaves accidentally fell into a pot of water he was boiling for consumption around 2700 B.C.E.

Alternative: After your initial straining of this beverage, place in a glass container with a screw top. Leave the top loose for several days while the wine works (bubbles will appear in one-quarter inch thickness on top of the liquid). When the bubbles almost disappear, turn the top tightly and leave for 24 hours then refrigerate. This yields almost a soda pop-like wine with very little alcohol.

LOVE AND ROMANCE

"God made man frail as a bubble,
god made love and love made trouble!"

—John Dryden

It's difficult, if not impossible, to maintain harmony in a relationship without healthy love. Similarly, adding a little romance into long-term relationships tends to keep things interesting and fresh. Thankfully one of the most popular tools in the Witch's kit was the love potion!

We have tons of historical examples from which to choose our components and methods. In particular, we can look to Catherine LaVoisin, the mistress of Louis XVI of France. She was known for her knowledge of magick potions, especially those for love, passion, and beauty. Many of the ingredients she used are listed below, and continue to be used today!

Magickal components for love and romance include:

dill	cinnamon	caraway
coriander	nutmeg	rose
fennel	celery	ginseng
parsley	apricot	leek
apple	basil	bay
cherry juice	chocolate	ginger
honey	kiwi	lavender
lemon	marjoram	orange
strawberry	tomato juice	vanilla

Definitely consider making these by candlelight or when the moon is full to set the right mood! Serve from a pink- or red-colored cup to accentuate your purpose further. For crystal tonics, turn to amethyst, onyx, beryl, and pink quartz.

Traditional Mulled Ale

2 cups ale	2 whole cloves
2 tsp. crushed fresh gingerroot	2 Tbs. butter
2 Tbs. sugar	2 eggs beaten

Directions: Place ale, clove, ginger, butter, and sugar into a large saucepan and bring to just boiling. Slowly pour this mixture into the beaten eggs, and then transfer into a large bottle. Pour this into another jug, repeating this several times to build up froth, then return to the pan to reheat. Remove ginger and cloves before serving hot.

Magickal Associations: Partnership, love, and romance.

History/Lore: A favorite Victorian treat, mulled ale is a warm, welcoming beverage for cold Winter nights in front of a romantic fire. The number two is employed throughout this recipe to encourage positive emotions and communications between two people.

Apricot Amour Nectar

1 lb. ripe apricots, blanched	1lb. dried apricots
1 cup apricot nectar	1 tsp. vanilla extract
1 qt. vodka	1 1/2 cups sugar

Directions: Slice and prick your whole apricots into eight pieces. Likewise prick the dried apricots. Place these equally dispersed in one-quart jars with half the vanilla in each. Next, warm the vodka only slightly so that the sugar can be dissolved in it. Pour half of this mixture into each jar, cover, and seal. This mixture should age three months, the liquid being served as a cordial and the fruits as a dessert with whipped cream.

Magickal Associations: The spirit of Amour!

History/Lore: Apricot is considered a love food being sacred to, and ruled by, Venus. It was a favored fruit on Elizabethan tables and thought to owe its origins to Western Asia.

Alternatives: To add a little fervor to this beverage, reduce apricot juice by half, then blend in half a cup of passion fruit juice.

Eros Tomatoes

1 gal. tomato juice	1/2 pkg. wine yeast
2 lbs. tomatoes	5 cups sugar

Directions: Dissolve the sugar in a small amount of the tomato juice, which has been warmed. Meanwhile, in another pot, place the tomatoes with the juice in a large pan bringing them to boil until soft (about seven minutes). Mash thoroughly, returning to simmer for about one hour, then strain as much liquid as possible out of the mixture. Blend this with the sugar juice and let sit overnight. In the morning, suspend your yeast in warm water for 15 minutes before stirring into the juice. Ferment for three weeks in a large container, then strain off the clearer liquid into bottles for aging. Ready in nine to 12 months.

Magickal Associations: Romance, protection, blood mysteries (note the coloration), vitality, passion, Fire magicks.

History/Lore: The tomato has its origins in the pre-Columbian regions of Central and South America where the cultures were largely vegetarian. The folk name for the tomato is the "love apple."

Romantic Roses

1 to 2 gal. pot filled 1/2 full with rose petals	1 gal. water
2 Tbsp. rose water	3 lbs. sugar
1/2 pkg. wine or champagne yeast	1 tsp. orange juice

Directions: Cover the rose petals with water and simmer over a low flame until the petals become see-through. Strain off the liquid, returning it to the original pan to warm with sugar until the sugar is dissolved. Cool to lukewarm, adding champagne yeast (preferably), which has been suspended in 1/4 cup warm water. Cover the pot with a cloth for 24 hours to begin fermentation. The next day, move the liquid to a large container with fitted fermentation lock and add the rose water and orange juice to it. Allow this to age until fermentation has all but ceased. Rack off the clear pink liquid by placing a siphon into the bottle about one inch above any sediment in the bottom. Transfer the clear liquid into bottles with a sugar cube in each bottle. Cork using champagne corks and store in dark, cool area for one month. Issue caution when opening, as bottles will have a fair amount of pressure built up.

Magickal Associations: The spirit of love and beauty.

History/Lore: Greeks considered the rose to be one of the best symbols of love and loveliness, having been born from the blood of Aphrodite. Romans often covered festival floors with roses in welcome to honored guests. Arabs call rose water the "dew of paradise."

Love Potion

6 small apples, sliced	1 gal. water
3 cups strawberries	1/8 tsp. ginger
2 oranges	1/8 tsp. cinnamon
2 small slices lemon peel	2 1/2 lbs. sugar
3 cups raspberries	1/3 pkg. yeast

Directions: Find deep red apples for this recipe and leave the skins on. These combined with the berries yields a deep red color to encourage love. Follow basic recipe for wine, removing oranges and lemon peel after liquid has cooled to lukewarm, and then continue as directed.

Magickal Associations: Spirited romance, dedication, fervor, compassion, sagacity.

History/Lore: All the herbs and fruits of this recipe have been chosen for their longstanding association with love. The number of fruit slices were chosen to represent partnership (2), the union of two people (3), and devotion to the relationship (6).

Violet Liaison

1 lemon, sliced   1 orange sliced
1 qt. spring water   2 whole cloves
1/2 cup packed violet petals

Directions: Place the first four ingredients in your simmering pan first. Heat the liquid until tepid, but not hot. Add the violets and simmer until they are almost see-through. Strain and serve hot or cold in one glass with two straws!

Magickal Associations: Romance, love, keeping a cool head and warm heart, protection in relationships.

History/Lore: Both violets and cloves are strongly associated with human passions; thus, in this recipe two singular cloves are used to symbolize a couple. When carried, cloves are thought to encourage romantic interest. Violets are under the zodiacal domain of Venus, symbolizing enchantment in the language of flowers.

Alternative: Try adding two chamomile tea bags to the simmering liquid to bring peace in a home where tensions have discouraged the spirit of romance.

Chocolate-Covered Cherries

1 8 oz. glass of cherry soda   1 Tbsp. chocolate syrup
1 tsp. cherry extract   1 Tbsp. malt extract
dash cinnamon   cherries (garnish)

Directions: Place ingredients together in a blender and whip until frothy. Pour into glass, sprinkling cinnamon on top and decorating with fresh cherries.

Magickal Associations: Sweet, romantic love. Please use two straws in one cup!

History/Lore: In lands to the east, the beautiful cherry tree has long been associated with amorous pursuits, and chocolate is a food that inspires passion in most people I know (if only for the chocolate itself!).

Alternative: For a lustier blend, add a little mint.

Vanilla Venus

2 cups vanilla coffee, chilled   1 cup soda water
3 scoops vanilla ice cream   1 tsp. vanilla extract
whipped cream

Directions: Another cold coffee drink, this is mixed most easily in a blender, leaving the whipped cream for a garnish on top. Serve in soda glasses.

Magickal Associations: Love, rituals honoring Venus or Aphrodite.

History/Lore: Vanilla is actually a member of the orchid family, grown in Mexico and Central America. Once discovered, it managed to topple rose water as the favored flavoring of Medieval Europe, and has been used widely as a magickal attractant for romance.

Alternative: Try adding some almond extract in place of vanilla. Magickally this still accentuates your goals while adding a lovely, light nutty flavor.

LUCK

"There are few sporting men who are not in the habit of wearing charms and talismans."

—Thorstein Veblen

Almost everything in life benefits from a little extra serendipity. In fact, you'd be hard pressed to find anyone who says they wouldn't like more luck! In magickal terms, luck boils down to a positive energy flow that attracts similar energy. In turn, good events—some unexpected and surprising—begin happening.

Mind you, when I speak of luck I'm not talking about winning a huge lottery. That gets into an "iffy" territory that borders on using our magick to fulfill greed. Instead, I think of finding an extra $10 bill on the street, getting a check in the mail when it's most needed, and running into the right people at the right time. That's the kind of good fortune these beverages are designed to inspire.

Some of the ingredients that bear lucky energy include:

allspice	apple	banana
basil	cherry	egg
heather	kiwi	nasturtium
onion	parsley	red beverages

The Moon drives luck's energy, so definitely make these during the waxing to full moon. For crystal potions use carnelian, holy stones, jade, and moonstone.

Honeysuckle Serendipity

4 cups honeysuckle blossoms	1 gal. water
6 cups sugar	2 oranges, sliced and juiced
1/2 pkg. wine yeast	

Directions: Place the blossoms in a large crock. Warm half the water to just below boiling, then pour over the petals. Allow to sit until blossoms turn almost translucent. Strain and re-warm slightly to add orange juice, pieces, and yeast. Place into a fermentation container with a lock until the liquid becomes clear. Bottle and store in cool dark area for use.

Magickal Associations: Luck, good fortune, and good health.

History/Lore: If you find a honeysuckle plant growing near your home (also known as Woodbine), it is not only a sign of good fortune, but also a protector of the family's health.

Fortune Draught

2 qts. dandelion blossoms	2 qts. clover blossoms
1 gal. boiling water	3 lbs. sugar
2 lemons	2 oranges
1/2 pkg. of yeast	1 cup raisins

Directions: Remove any stems and leaves from your blossoms, placing them in a large cooking pot. Pour the boiling water over top of these, adding sugar, sliced lemon, and oranges. Simmer for a half-hour, then cool to lukewarm. Add the wine yeast suspended as shown in other recipes herein, stir. This should sit covered with a loosely woven cloth for one week

Magickal Associations: Luck, opportunity, and windfalls.

History/Lore: Dandelions acquire their name from the jagged leaves, which resemble lion's teeth (note the French term *dent de lion*). This gives this beverage a bit of a protective bite. More importantly, however, is the association both clovers and dandelions hold for luck. A four-leaf clover is considered most fortunate, as is dreaming of a dandelion.

Good Luck Clovers

1 tsp. dried clover flowers   1 tsp. daisy petals
1 cup hot water   honey to taste
1 daisy bud with leaf (garnish)

Directions: Place the petals in a gauze wrap or tea ball and steep for 15 minutes. Remove and flavor with honey. The daisy bud should be snipped so that it barely appears over the edge of your cup, like a young spring sprout.

History/Lore: The daisy is a flower that represents youthful innocence and wishes. Clover enhances this with a bit of luck and the power of protection to keep our goals plausible.

Alternatives: A stick of cinnamon can replace the daisy garnish in this recipe for successful energies.

Coffee Karma

2 scoops cappuccino ice cream   1 cup chocolate ice cream
1/2 cup dark roast coffee, cold   1/4 cup cream
grated dark chocolate

Directions: A marvelously easy beverage to make, all your ingredients, except one teaspoon of the cream, are placed in a blender and mixed until smooth. Serve by pouring into a glass with the teaspoon of cream on top and chocolate shavings for garnish.

Magickal Associations: Rewarding good actions, fortune that comes from your own efforts, delight.

History/Lore: To be honest, this recipe is not so much magickal as it is personally pleasing and downright decadent. The rich flavor brings a smile to the face of any coffee or chocolate lover I know.

Hazelnut Windfall

4 eggs	3/4 cup sugar
2 cups milk	1 cup hazelnut coffee
1 Tbs. hazelnut extract	1 cup cream

Directions: Beat eggs and sugar together until thick and frothy. Add milk and coffee, which have been warmed together with extract slowly to the sugar mixture. Separately beat heavy cream and gradually mix one tablespoon of this into each cup as it is poured. Serve warm.

Magickal Associations: Fertility, wisdom, and luck.

History/Lore: A favorite wood for dowsers, hazel trees offer their fruit for a number of other magickal applications, including increasing fundicity and as gifts to a young bride for joy in her new life.

Luck of the Irish

1 tsp. sugar or honey	2 Tbs. whipped cream
1/2 cup Irish whiskey	2 drops green coloring
1/2 cup black coffee	2 Tbs. heavy cream

Directions: Mix honey, whiskey, and black coffee together in a large cup. Float the heavy cream on top and then add a mound of whipped cream, which has been tinted green—the color of shamrocks!

Magickal Associations: Serendipity, good fortune, and godsends.

History/Lore: The Irish claim to be the most fortuitous people on the Earth, with the shamrock and Blarney stone to aid them. This coffee is a favorite beverage there and has become quite popular abroad.

Alternatives: For a more Scottish tone, leave the whipped cream white and use drambuis in place of the whiskey. Magickally speaking, this is for hospitality.

Grapes of Grandure

1 gal. grape juice	2 cups honeysuckle blossoms
1 1/2 cups orange juice	1 jasmine tea bag
1/4 cup honey	

Directions: Place all your ingredients together in a large pot for simmering. Warm very slowly over low flame until honey is fully dissolved. If your petals turn translucent before the honey is mixed, remove them and continue warming. Cool to room temperature, strain, and chill. Shake well before serving.

Magickal Associations: Awareness (especially psychic), good fortune, financial stability, protection of health, friendship.

History/Lore: Also known as woodbine, in the language of flowers honeysuckle symbolizes brotherly affection. It is featured in the Old Testament as the third flower in the Song of Solomon. In the Middle Ages, a syrup of honeysuckle was used to fight fever.

Alternative: I like this prepared simply with warm water or apple juice in place of the grape. With apple, this beverage is magickally appropriate for wisdom in relationships or with regard to personal resources.

MAGICK

*"The magick of the tongue is the
most dangerous of all spells."*
—Edward Bulwer Lytton

What would a book of Witch's beverages and brews be without a few laced with magick! How can you use them? Lots of ways! Drink one to increase the power of a spell. Try another to help manifest your personal vision of the magickal arts and increase your aptitude. Quaff another still when you just want to feel witchier!

Serve magickally oriented brews from a silver cup, the color of the moon (it was once believed that Witches got their power from the lunar sphere!). If possible, prepare them in a cauldron, the legs of which represent the threefold God/Goddess. And, should you be feeling *really* witchy, go ahead and cackle while you work...think of it like whistling with an attitude!

Some of the ingredients associated with magick and magickal power include:

chrysanthemums	vanilla	carnation
rosemary	tea	mint
rose	ginger	echinacea
pineapple	coffee	citron
honey	rum	red and purple beverages

Prepare these beverages during the full moon. Or, perhaps prepare them at a time suited to your specific goals magickally. For example, if you're hoping to apply yourself to magickal studies, you might wish to do it during the daytime hours of the full moon so the conscious, learning self is stressed along with the intuitive nature. For crystal elixirs look to malachite, bloodstone, and quartz.

Four Quarter Harmony

1 cup diced quince (Earth)	1 cup mulberries (Air)
1 orange, peeled and sectioned (Fire)	1 large apple, diced (Water)
	1 qt. vodka
2/3 cup honey	1/8 tsp. cinnamon
1/8 tsp. ginger	

Directions: Place the fruits in a large crock with vodka and allow to soak for four to five hours. Mix in the honey and spices next, covering the crock securely. A flower and water paste over the edges helps to keep flavor, aroma, and alcohol content at a good level. Place the entire mixture in the oven at 200 degrees for 10 hours. Cool and strain, serving either hot or cold.

Magickal Associations: Balance, symmetry, and accord. Casting the magick circle.

History/Lore: Each of the four fruits chosen in this recipe correspond, with one quarter of the magick circle (one element). Just as in magick, combining each element in harmony produces some powerful, and in this instance tasty, results! This particular recipe comes from the Ukraine.

Alternatives: If you can not readily find quince, feel free to substitute fresh or canned pears (in juice, not syrup).

Mystic Bowl

1/2 gal. apple juice	3 broken peppermint sticks
1 cup sugar	2 cups soda water
2 cups whiskey	3 broken cinnamon sticks

Directions: Using two cups of apple juice over a low flame, dissolve the sugar. Mix this with the rest of the juice and pour into punch bowl with whiskey and spices. Allow this to sit covered for a half hour before chilling, and then add soda water just before serving.

Magickal Associations: Occult insight and ability; magickal talents being manifest.

History/Lore: During the time of the Greek gods, to own an apple tree was to posses supernatural powers. Cinnamon and peppermint enhance this energy.

Mulberry Magus

1 gal. water	1/2 lemon, sliced
3 lbs. sugar	1/3 pkg. yeast
5 lbs. mulberries	1/2" slice bruised gingerroot

Directions: Place your mulberries with the water and mash them, leaving to set overnight. Follow the basic recipe, allowing open-air fermentation for one week, followed by a straining, then another week of open-air working. Pour into glass containers to let sit for three more weeks, then strain again into final containers. This should age two years for best flavor.

Magickal Associations: Magickal transformation of energies, enlightenment.

History/Lore: The Chinese hold this berry in such fervent regard as to believe it can eliminate the need for food and eventually transform the consumer into a being of light!

Orange Oracle

2 small lemons	1 gal. water
2 medium oranges	1/4 tsp. yeast
1 cup raisins	2 cups brown sugar

Directions: Peel the fruit, setting aside the rind. Using a fine knife or fork, remove as much of the white membrane as you can from both the fruit and rind. Slice the lemons and limes into a large bowl with the sugar and cleaned fruit skins. Pour the boiling water over it, allowing to cool to lukewarm. Next, add your yeast as directed in general recipe for wine, allowing open-air fermentation for 24 hours. Finally, place your raisins in the bottom of a bottle and pour the liquid into it, *capping tightly.* Continue to allow the beverage to ferment at room temperature until the raisins move to the top of the bottle, then refrigerate for use. Please note that this wine has the extra advantage of a very mild alcohol content.

Magickal Associations: Vision, predictions, magickal and oracular power.

History/Lore: In Finland wines like this one are called Sima. The citrus fruits add precision to your magickal efforts, and raisins are thought to help encourage psychic dreams.

Cinnamon and Sorcery

5 cups hot apple juice
3/4 cup sugar
1/2 cup orange juice
2 sticks cinnamon

10 apple tea bags
juice of one lemon
6 cloves

Directions: Warm the apple juice in a large saucepan over a medium flame. Add the apple tea bags and allow to steep for at least 15 minutes before removing. Next add sugar, juice, and spices. Allow to simmer for another 10 minutes. This can then be poured into a punch bowl and served hot, with cinnamon sticks for cup garnishes.

Magickal Associations: Wise use of magickal power.

History/Lore: Cinnamon is a power herb, while apple juice encourages thoughtfulness in how we use our gifts.

Berry Blessings

3 whole strawberries
6 raspberries
1 tsp. sugar
6 oz. skim milk

6 blueberries
10 black berries
1 Tbsp. malt extract
2 oz. soda water

Directions: Rinse your fruit thoroughly, then blend all ingredients together until frothy. Serve as is or over ice. Please note that sundae sauces can be used in lieu of fresh fruit; about half a teaspoon is all that's necessary.

Magickal Associations: Learning magickal arts.

History/Lore: When properly prepared, this malted comes out a lovely violet hue, the color most commonly associated with spiritual pursuits and metaphysical learning.

Alternative: Consider floating a fresh violet on top of this drink to further accent the magickal energies. These flowers are often grown in the home to promote sacred pursuits.

PEACE AND REST

"If we have no peace it is because we have forgotten that we belong to each other"

—Mother Teresa

Considering the hectic pace of most people's lives, I can think of no one who couldn't use a sense of inner peace and calm. In fact, I truly believe this is a key component to a healthy, happy, spiritual life. If we never slow down, if we're never quiet and still, we cannot hear the voice of the Sacred whispering to us.

Then too, our world is filled with strife, of person-to-person fighting and struggle. The reason varies, but the result is the same: the desperate need for global pace. Witches recognize that even this somewhat grand-sounding goal begins with each individual being comfortable with her place in the greater scheme and having true inner harmony. So that's where the beverages in this chapter begin.

The common components for peace include:

basil	lavender	lettuce
blue drinks	white drinks (truce)	water
catnip	quince	cumin
rose	violet	marigold
saffron	marjoram	oregano
cucumber	apple	peach
passion fruit	raspberry	apricot

Timing for these beverages depends on your goal. If you are seeking a good night's rest, I'd suggest preparing your drink just before bed. If you're trying to settle an overactive emotional system that's disrupting inner peace, prepare it in the daylight. And, if you're making a libation aimed at inspiring world peace, I'd seriously consider making it on the night of a blue moon—we can use a miracle or two in that area!

For crystal tinctures, use amethyst, aventurine, carnelian, malachite, obsidian, or sodalite.

Inner Peace Potable

4 qts. water	1 1/2 cups sugar
1/4 cup nettle leaves	1/2 cup brown sugar
1" bruised gingerroot	1 pkg. beer yeast
1/2 tsp. grated lemon peel	sugar cubes
1/2 tsp. grated orange peel	

Directions: Place the nettle leaves with ginger, lemon peel, and orange peel in water. Bring to a boil, and then lower heat to simmer for a half hour. Strain. To this add sugars, stirring until totally dissolved. Cool the liquid until lukewarm. While you are waiting, suspend the beer yeast in a quarter cup warm water. Add this to the spiced water and let work in a warm area with a cloth over it until all signs of bubbling seem to stop. Strain again while bottling, adding two sugar cubes to each quart bottle. Let this sit closed securely for seven days before drinking. Shelf life is another two to three weeks.

Magickal Associations: Grace, peace of mind, seclusion.

History/Lore: Versions of spiced small beers appear in many lands, specifically to this recipe, Wales, a country known for its beauty and solitude.

Alternatives: For a beer with more cleansing qualities, try adding a teaspoonful of freshly ground grapefruit rind and two fruit slices during the boiling. For fuller flavor, substitute honey for sugar in the same proportions. Test this, as sometimes more sweetness may be desired to offset the grapefruit.

Harmonic Draught

2 cups boiling water	white flower (garnish)
1/2 cup sugar	1 jigger gin
9 mint leaves	slice of lemon

Directions: Stir sugar into the boiling water until it is totally dissolved. Steep the mint leaves and lemon for about 10 minutes then remove adding gin. May also be chilled and served. Garnish.

Magickal Associations: Peace, serenity, and reconciliation.

History/Lore: Nine is the number of universal law and symmetry. Mint has been honored with such folk names as "heart mint" and "lamb mint" as an indication of its peaceful nature. Greeks and Romans often used mint in baths to help calm tensions. The white flower is added as an emblem of amicable intentions.

Restful Pleasure

3 cups boiling water   1 ltr. brandy
12 quinces, peeled and diced
2 chamomile tea bags

Directions: Place the quince and chamomile in the boiling water in a large bowl. Allow to sit until cool. To this, add the liter of brandy and store together in an airtight container for three months. Strain. May be served warm with a cinnamon stick or chilled over ice.

Magickal Associations: Accord, restfulness, relaxed visits with friends, serenity.

History/Lore: To the ancient Greeks, the quince was a fruit that insured joy and harmony, especially in relationships. They sometimes called it the "golden apple," much as they did the orange. Chamomile likewise encourages this tranquility.

Amendment Wine

1 lb. sweet almonds   2 lbs. sugar
1 tsp. cinnamon   1 pint cherry juice
2 tsp. almond extract   1 gal. water
1/2 oz orange blossom water   1/3 pkg. yeast
    (optional)   pinch of lemon rind

Directions: Finely crush the sweet almonds. Meanwhile, bring one half of your water to boil, then pour this over the almonds. Let the nuts soak for 48 hours, then move to the stove and follow basic recipe.

Magickal Associations: Restoring relationships, reconciliation, and forgiveness.

History/Lore: This recipe has its origins in Russia, where like many European lands, orange water symbolizes faithfulness. Almond is employed with this for energy.

Truce Mead

1 gal. apple cider   1 1/2 lbs. grapes

Directions: Follow the instructions for non-alcoholic mead, except that your cider replaces the one gallon of water in the basic recipe. Additionally, I suggest using seedless grapes that have been mashed to extract the greatest amount of juice.

Magickal Associations: Offerings for peace among people. In a group setting, this should be shared from a communal cup.

History/Lore: Here we have combined a cider-like beverage popular in Europe and this recipe, which is reminiscent of an ancient wine from Egypt known as Pymeat, for a truly international drink to encourage a one-world perspective.

Alternatives: Choose your grapes according to your goals. White can be for harmony and purity, or purple for spiritual insight.

Chamomile Comfort

1 cup boiling water   1 cup hopped beer
1 chamomile tea bag   honey to taste
1/2 tsp. lavender   1/2 tsp. lemon verbena

Directions: Place the lavender and lemon verbena in a tea ball or gauze cloth. Steep these with the chamomile in the boiling water for 10 minutes. Meanwhile, warm the beer to a palatable temperature, while stirring in honey. Blend these in equal proportions with the tea and enjoy two cups full. Especially useful just before bed.

Magickal Associations: Peacefulness, tranquility, gentility, and consolation.

History/Lore: Chamomile is known for its sedative quality. The scent of lavender helps calm the nerves; lemon verbena helps encourage rest; and hops improves sleep.

Tea Time at Trish's

1 tsp. mint tea	2 cinnamon sticks
1 tsp. apple tea	1/4 cup honey
1 tsp. berry tea	orange peel (fresh)
1 tsp. black tea	lemon peel (fresh)
4 cups boiling water	2 tsp. lemon juice

Directions: Steep the four types of tea in hot water using a tea ball or bag, then remove tea. While hot, add your cinnamon, honey, fruit rinds (one whole fruit each), and lemon juice. This is wonderful hot, or may be chilled and served over chipped ice.

Magickal Associations: Relaxation, healthy leisure, and introspection, which rejuvenates.

History/Lore: Tea was one of the plants sacred to Buddha, and considering all its uses in religion and medicine, it is certainly no wonder. During the Victorian Era, it was often associated with the pleasurable moments of quiet sharing with friends.

Cool-Off Coffee

4 ice cubes crushed	1 to 2 Tbsp. sugar
4 cups strong coffee	1 tsp. amaretto flavoring
(your choice)	amaretto whipped cream

Directions: Place the crushed ice with sugar, coffee, and flavoring in a blender on medium speed for two to three minutes. Pour into a tall glass or cup and top off with whipped cream. Most supermarkets now stock the amaretto flavored aerosol cream, or you can make it fresh and simply add one teaspoon extract during the beating process.

Magickal Associations: Calming energies, cooling tempers.

History/Lore: The icy nature of this beverage puts a distinctive chill on emotions or energy that has gotten out of control.

Consolation Cup

1 cup chamomile flowers	1 cup passion fruit juice
1 cup spearmint leaves	1/2 cup hop flowers
dash fennel	

Directions: Use one teaspoon of this mixture to one cup of warmed passion fruit juice, steeped for 10 minutes and strained. Chill, then if desired, add a bit of heavy cream, plain or whipped.

Magickal Associations: Solace, serenity, peacefulness.

History/Lore: This is actually a very practical preparation that helps ease tension and stress. Hops helps to bring drowsiness. Once sleep is obtained, spearmint is thought to help protect against nightmares and negativity. The Greeks referred to chamomile as "Apple of the Earth."

Alternative: Lavender can be substitute for spearmint in the proportion of three-quarters of a cup. This is strongly recommended for people experiencing spiritual depression or discouragement.

PROTECTION

*"Beneath the shadow of great protection the soul sits,
hushed and calm"*

—James F. Clarke

The world is not always a safe place. All around us dangers exist, from a simple cold bug and distracted people driving cars, to thievery and other criminal activity! Danger can also exist on a spiritual level; such as the energy caused by negative thought forms or the disturbances caused by an ill-spirited ghost!

It has always been my stance that in all such matters forewarned is forearmed. We need to practice proactive protective magick, and beverages help us do just that. Because you consume these (for the most part) you then carry the protective energy with you wherever you may be. And, should you wish a little extra safety in your personal space, all you need do is sprinkle a bit of the same beverage around. This particular approach usually works better when combined with visualization and/or incantations to strengthen the effect.

Some of the ingredients commonly used for protective magick include:

banana	basil	bay
dill	garlic	ice
marjoram	peach	pepper
radish	red juices/wines	anise
white beverages	blueberry	coconut
cinnamon	ginseng	beer
heather	chrysanthemum	citrus
mulberry	papaya	raspberry
rhubarb	rose	sage
clove	rosemary	plum
almond flavoring	walnut flavoring	

Bear in mind this list is very abbreviated. Protective magick often changes depending on what kind of protection you needed. A beverage to keep ghosts away might include garlic, for example, while one to protect you from depression might include marjoram.

You have no time constraints on protective magick. Do it when you *need* it (and perhaps even before you need it!). For crystal elixirs use amber, cat's eye, holy stones, lapis, obsidian, and/or turquoise.

Protection Potion

2 Tbsp. anise	1 qt. warm water
2 Tbsp. fennel	1 cup sugar
2" strip of lemon peel	1 tsp. yeast

Directions: Place the anise, fennel, and finely sliced bits of the lemon peel in the water and allow to soak for one hour. Strain and return the water to a low flame, adding sugar and stirring until dissolved. While this cools to lukewarm, suspend the yeast in one-quarter cup warm water. Mix into the tea-like water, then bottle with a loose cork for about 10 days. Slowly tighten cork, then age until liquid in bottle looks clear (about three months).

Magickal Associations: Cleansing, turning negativity, safety from malevolent magick.

History/Lore: Anise has been used since the time of Virgil to protect against the evil eye. Fennel mirrors this in medieval Europe, where it was rubbed on the body to keep mischievous Witchcraft away.

Samhain Safety

1 large pumpkin   brown sugar to fill
1 ltr. rum   1 orange, juiced
3 to 5 cloves (optional)

Directions: Clean out all the seeds from the inside of the pumpkin, leaving the insides intact and carefully preserving the lid. Fill the central cavity with brown sugar mixed with rum and the orange juice. Cloves are likewise added now if desired. Reseal the pumpkin using a little wax around the edges of the lid. Hang from the ceiling over a bowl using some netting for three weeks or until juice begins to leak from the bottom of the pumpkin. Make a hole in the bottom and release the rest of the juice, straining into bottles and allowing to age for one month before using.

Magickal Associations: Protection and safety from ghosts.

History/Lore: Long before they became a welcome feature to Samhain and Thanksgiving celebrations, pumpkins were known in the New World as "pumpions." Slowly, they replaced turnips as the choice carving vegetable for Halloween to keep wandering spirits away.

Bubbling Brewpot

5 cups fresh raspberries	1 orange sliced thinly
1 ltr. gin	mint leaves (garnish)
1 orange, juiced	5 tsp. sugar
1/2 ltr. raspberry ginger ale	

Directions: Crush five cups of the raspberries and place them in the punch bowl. Add gin, the juice of the one orange, and sugar, beating with a wire whisk. Next add ginger ale, floating sliced orange and mint on top. Serve with ice for eight people.

Magickal Associations: Protection, especially from wandering Spirits; boldness in the face of adversity.

History/Lore: No toil and trouble here! In the Philippines, raspberry vines are regarded as very protective. They are often draped near a doorway shortly after a loved one's death to keep an unsettled ghost from entering. One wonders if this early connotation of safety eventually lead to the idea of "giving a raspberry" as a sign of defiance—in this case even of the afterlife!

Blackberry Bramble

1/4 tsp. angelica root	1/4 tsp. dill seed
1/8 tsp. horehound	1/2 tsp. fennel
1/2 cup warmed blackberry wine	1/2 cup hot water
	3 to 4 whole blackberries

Directions: Place your herbs in a tea ball to steep in the half cup of hot water for 20 minutes. To this, add your blackberry wine and a few whole berries as a garnish. Honey may be added for sweetening if desired. A good beverage to enjoy before bed.

Magickal Associations: Protection from negative magicks, purification, and atonement.

History/Lore: Horehound is one of the five bitter herbs of Passover. It was also used predominantly in Europe to cure cases thought to be caused by a magickal toxin. Hyssop was similarly lauded for cleansing: in the words of David, "Purge me with Hyssop, and I shall be clean."

Sparkling Sanctuary

2 bottles sparkling white grape juice
1 12-oz. can pineapple with syrup   1" bruised gingerroot

Directions: Drain the syrup from the pineapple and place in a small pan with one tablespoon of water. Add gingerroot and warm for 15 minutes. Strain off root. Pour this liqueur into the grape juice and garnish with fresh green grapes or pineapple chunks.

Magickal Associations: Protection.

History/Lore: Both ginger and pineapple are considered to be protective, the first because of its biting flavor and the second because of its prickly exterior.

Mettle Nettle

2 cups of well-washed nettles   1/2" gingerroot, bruised
3 medium potatoes, poked   1 gal. water
brown sugar to taste

Directions: Boil the potatoes for one hour in the water, then strain. Add nettles and gingerroot, returning the liquid to the stove for an additional hour. Strain again and add sugar to taste. Best served warm.

Magickal Associations: New perspectives, cleansing, protection.

History/Lore: A beverage great for a good energy boost and attitude improvement, this drink is high in minerals. Nettle sometimes slows bleeding when applied to skin and was once worn as an amulet to protect against evil spirits.

PSYCHISM AND AWARENESS

"A soul without watchfulness is like a city without walls."
—William Secker

Not all Witches are psychic and not all psychics are Witches! For those of us who fall into the first category, beverages that enhance supernatural senses or "tune in" spiritual comprehension skills are very helpful to magickal efforts. For example, if you're not aware that there is some negative energy heading your way, you're far less likely to protect yourself from it. Psychism prepares you for what's ahead, while awareness helps with nearly every part of life of which I can think!

Here are some ingredients commonly used to enhance either of these attributes:

bay	celery	cinnamon
nutmeg	dandelion	rose
thyme	sprouts	coconut
purple juices	clover	fennel

For crystal tinctures, turn to amethyst, beryl, citrine, lapis, and the ever-faithful clear quartz.

Consider making your psychic drinks during a full moon, the symbol that represents our superconscious and magickal nature. Awareness brews can be made at the same time, but if you're looking for conscious awareness you might want to consider making them at noon during a day when the full moon is present. This will provide you with the best of both worlds (solar and lunar energy). Serve them in a silver cup, the color of our insightful nature.

By the way, you can dab a bit of this liquid on your third eye or temples to symbolically activate the energy in areas associated with those traits. The third eye is often considered the psychic center (between your eyebrows) and your temples are a "thinking" zone.

Seer's Beer

1/2 qt. dandelion flowers	1/2" gingerroot, bruised
1/2 lemon, diced finely	2 qts. water
1 cup brown sugar	1/4 cup white sugar
1/8 cup cream of tartar	1/8 oz. beer yeast (top fermenting)

Directions: Wash your dandelion flowers, then place them in a large pot along with the ginger, lemon, and water. Boil this together for 15 minutes. In another large container, mix the sugars and cream of tartar together, slowly pouring in the hot liquid to dissolve. Strain and allow to cool to lukewarm.

Meanwhile, suspend the yeast in one-quarter cup warm water. Add this to the cooled liquid to begin fermentation. Keep in a warm place with a heavy cloth over top for three days before straining and bottling. Age for one week, then enjoy. Shelf life on this is short—about six weeks before it gets very bitter.

Magickal Association: Prophesy, psychic visions, dream oracles

History/Lore: The most loved and hated plant of all time, dandelions are rich in vitamins and minerals. They mark the sun's movement by closing their petals when it is dark, symbolize ancient prognostication, and were often used for love augury.

Carrot Keen

1 gal. water
1 lb. raisins, chopped
1/2 pkg. wine yeast
4 lbs. carrots
4 cups brown sugar, lightly packed

Directions: Boil the chopped, cleaned carrots in water until very tender. Strain, retaining carrots for use in carrot cake. Return the liquid to the pan, adding sugar, stirring until totally dissolved. Place raisins in a large fermenting jar with suspended yeast mixture and pour lukewarm carrot juice over top. Use a fermentation lock or balloon for three weeks until fermentation is complete. Strain into another jug with secure lid allowing to age another two months before bottling the clear fluid at top.

Magickal Associations: Keen insight, heightened inner vision, and alertness.

History/Lore: In Scotland, carrots participate in a holiday known as Carrot Sunday, when this vegetable is gathered, blessed at the churches, and taken home to protect the household. Anyone finding a forked carrot is considered doubly fortunate and safeguarded. Meanwhile, mothers everywhere recommend eating carrots to improve your "sight."

Petaled Oracle

1 qt. apple wine
2 oranges
1 cup sugar

2 limes
8 rose geranium leaves

Directions: Warm the apple wine, sugar, and geranium for five to 10 minutes until sugar is dissolved. Add sliced limes and oranges and allow to cool. Strain and bottle, aging for one month before consuming.

Magickal Associations: Prophesy, insight, using divination as a service to others.

History/Lore: This beverage comes to us from Arabia, where the prophet Mahomet is given honor as birthing this lovely blossom. Some cunning folk of old would plant specially enchanted geraniums by their door to prepare them for impending guests by foreseeing their arrival.

Alternatives: Geraniums can be replaced with 6 whole bay leaves for similar magickal results.

Apricot Awareness

1 cup hot water
1 apricot or orange tea bag
1 tsp. apricot jam

1/2 cup apricot brandy
whipped cream (garnish)

Directions: Prepare your tea as usual, adding the apricot jam while still very hot in order to dissolve it. Pour in your brandy, then top with a tablespoon full of whipped cream. Sugar may be added for sweetening if desired.

Magickal Associations: Divination, foresight, sagacity, psychic awareness.

History/Lore: The Chinese regard the apricot tree as one of great prophetic power because it was here that Confucius wrote his commentaries. Additionally, one of the great religious minds of China, Lao-tse, was purportedly born under an apricot tree, already cognizant at birth.

Truth Tell

1 cup coconut
  (or coconut milk)
1 tsp. rum extract

1 cup pineapple juice
3 tsp. sugar
crushed ice

Directions: Canned coconut cream seems to work best for this beverage, having an already smooth texture. Thoroughly mix in unsweetened pineapple juice, sugar, and rum extract. Serve over crushed ice.

Magickal Associations: Protection from falsehood; improved awareness of deceptive images, especially on a psychic level.

History/Lore: Both the pineapple and coconut are associated with protective and psychic magick.

Alternative: Add a few strawberries to this drink to help you remove your rose-colored glasses pertaining to a romantic partner. In this instance, honey might be a better choice over sugar.

Psychic Physic

1 gal. water
6-10 whole fresh mint leaves
1/2 cup hop flowers
1 lb. sugar

4 cups fresh dandelion flowers
1/2 lemon, diced
1 mint tea bag
1/4 pkg. active yeast

Directions: Boil together the first six ingredients for 25 minutes and strain. Add sugar immediately thereafter, stirring in suspended yeast when liquid cools. Follow as per other recipes this section for bottling.

Magickal Associations: Growing awareness, improved clarity of psychic gifts, vision, foresight.

History/Lore: Oliver Wendell Homes said that these flowers leapt from the kindling Sun's fire, and they did so with a bounty, as any Spring lawn will show. In the language of flowers, they are symbolic of ancient oracles.

Foresight Fountain

2 cups cheery juice	1 cup orange juice
1 cup pomegranate juice	1 tsp. hazel extract
1/2 ltr. ginger ale or soda water	dandelion or broom flowers (garnish)

Directions: Pour your first four ingredients together and chill well before placing in punch bowl. Add ginger ale and float the flowers, after washing them well, atop the dish.

Magickal Associations: Psychic energy, improved insight, foresight, prophesy.

History/Lore: Each ingredient, with the exception of ginger ale, in this beveragehas at one time been linked with the ability to divine information. The soda adds bubbly energy to your efforts.

Alternatives: Try changing your garnish to reflect the goals of the question being asked. For love, use rose petals, or in matters of weather, float heather.

SENSUALITY AND SEXUALITY

"True sexuality acknowledges both these dimensions [spiritual and physical], and tries to embrace them both in the act of love."

—Kent Nerburn

Generally speaking, humans are not built for a hermetic existence. We are social beings that want to feel appreciated and express our feelings to others. For hundreds of thousands of years, a huge portion of this expression came in the form of procreation simply to continue the species. Modern Witches aren't quite that clinical about sex and sensuality. We see the body as a sacred gift, and one that should be enjoyed fully by mutually consenting adults.

A Witch's Beverages and Brews

That having been said, AIDS and other sexually transmitted diseases have created an atmosphere in which caution is certainly called for in our interpersonal expressions. This means that sensual, sexual brews should be created cautiously and with real mindfulness (as mindful as the act of lovemaking should be as well!). The idea in creating these beverages is to inspire yourself and your partner toward creatively communicating physical feelings that may have grown apathetic, dull, sluggish, static, or seem dead compared to that old spark you knew so well.

Some of the common magickal components used to nurture passion along include:

carrot	celery	cherry
chocolate	cinnamon	honey
nutmeg	peach	potato
raspberry	rose	strawberry
vanilla	mint	licorice
blackberry	papaya	mango
barley (beer)	rice milk	plums
rum	chartreuse	brandy

If preparing this beverage for a man, I suggest doing so during the day. The sun supports masculine energy. For women, just the opposite is true. Prepare the beverage by moonlight, especially that of a waxing moon, so sexual pleasure grows. For a crystal elixir, I recommend carnelian.

Woman's Wonder

1 qt. milk	1 small cinnamon stick
1 1/2 cups sugar	4 egg whites
1 tsp. lemon juice	1 cup cinnamon liqueur
2" piece lemon peel	

Directions: Place your milk in a small pan with one cup of sugar. Add lemon peel and cinnamon stick while simmering over low flame for about three to five minutes. Cool, strain, and set in freezer. Meanwhile, beat your eggwhites with a half-cup of sugar, adding lemon juice when peaks form. Beat this mixture into the chilled milk very slowly with equal portions of the cinnamon liqueur. Return to the freezer until a slush-like consistency forms. Serve in chilled glasses.

Magickal Associations: Improved potency, passion, and fervent energy (especially for women).

History/Lore: In the 1500s Arabic, camel caravans would arrive at European markets bearing many spices, including cinnamon, which they knew would fetch a handsome price. In Chinese mythology, cinnamon was the spice of immortality. Magickally, cinnamon is ruled by Venus and is considered a Fire herb, making it an excellent aphrodisiac.

Alternative: For success and prosperity, substitute one inch of bruised gingerroot and ginger liqueur for the cinnamon in this recipe.

God Aspect

1/2 cup crushed almonds	1 tsp. nutmeg
1/2 cup crushed cashews	1 whole walnut, per person
1/2 cup crushed hazelnuts	1 pint vodka
1 pint almond liqueur	

Directions: Place the first six ingredients together in a large glass container with lid for two months in the sunlight, shaking daily. Strain. Add almond liqueur and test for sweetness. Add honey if desired. Note that although this beverage is quite tasty without the almond liqueur, this last ingredient serves to accent the magickal aspects and improve flavor.

Magickal Associations: The huntsman, male virility and sexuality, Pan, The Horned One and other fertile god images.

History/Lore: Nuts in general have often been associated as an emblem of male sexuality. An old Phrygian tale tells about how one of their great gods, Attis, was born from an almond nut placed in the heart of the Goddess.

Creativity Cooler

1 ltr. peach brandy or liqueur   1 cup milk
6 ice cubes, chopped   2 Tbsp. heavy cream
1 banana, sliced

Directions: Place the brandy, milk, and ice together in a blender. Whip until frothy. Pour into glasses topped with a thin layer of heavy cream and sliced bananas for garnish.

Magickal Associations: Sexual symmetry and inventiveness.

History/Lore: The banana and peaches in this recipe combine to create a harmonious balance of male-female energies perfect to bring fertile energy into any creative effort or physical expression.

Banana Split Spritz

1 pint of your favorite ice cream   1 cup soda water or ginger ale
1 banana, sliced   2 tsp. maraschino cherry juice
2 tsp. of your favorite topping   whipped cream (garnish)
1 cherry (garnish)   sprinkles (garnish)

Directions: Place ice cream and a half-cup of the ginger ale in the blender on low setting. Slowly add the remaining pop with the other ingredients except garnishes. You may need to add more ginger ale to achieve a smooth enough texture to drink. Don't forget to put it in a large glass with two straws! This is definitely a beverage for sharing.

Magickal Associations: Love towards self and others, spiritual compassion, sexual pleasure.

History/Lore: Banana splits bring out the romantic idealist in almost everyone. In India, the banana leaf was a predominant part of marriage rites. In Polynesia, the banana plant figures heavily into legends, and in some areas banana plants are thought to encourage luck. The cherry on top of this creation also encourages love, being ruled by Venus.

Ice Cream Playfulness

1 qt. passion fruit juice	2 cups pineapple puree
1 qt. rainbow sherbet	1 ltr. ginger ale
1/2 ltr. vodka	2 cups whole cherries

Directions: Mix passion fruit with pineapple puree until well incorporated. Next, using a hand mixer, beat together the sherbet slightly softened, ginger ale, and vodka. Slowly mix this blend with the juice and pour into your punch bow. Float cherries on top. Makes about three and a half quarts.

Magickal Associations: Young love, exuberant passion, sexual playfulness, romance, adoration.

History/Lore: The combination of tropical fruit and ice cream makes a powerful vehicle for the imagination and flights of fancy, especially with regard to relationships. All the fruits included here have, at some time, been magickally associated with love.

Strawberry-Banana Stimulation

1 banana	1 cup plain yogurt
1 cup milk	5 strawberries
1 tsp. honey	pinch of ginger or cinnamon (optional)

Directions: Blend together the first five ingredients until well incorporated. Ladies pour this into a brandy-style glass, men into a long, champagne-style one. As you drink, envision the energy moving to "pleasure" centers to help encourage sexual enjoyment.

Magickal Associations: Sexual potency, stamina, fertility, fecundity, physical pleasure.

History/Lore: This is an especially nice beverage to try just before conception rites, or for people who are having problems enjoying physical contact. Plain yogurt encourages the spiritual nature, while the banana is representative of male energy and strawberry is the female.

Cherry Almond Delight

1 12-oz. can frozen cherry juice	1 slice orange
1 lb. pitted cherries	1 tea bag
6 cups apricot nectar	1 1/2 gal. water
2 1/2 Tbsp. sugar	1/3 pkg. yeast
1/2 tsp. almond extract	

Directions: Follow basic wine recipe, allowing a two-day open-air fermentation before straining off fruit. Please note that cherries exhibit a slow, steady fermentation.

Magickal Associations: Productivity, love magick, sexual equilibrium, and harmony.

History/Lore: As early as 8 B.C., herbalists in the region of Assyria were acclaiming the cherry for its wonderful smell and value to health. Magickally, cherries, apricots, and almonds are all associated with the energy of love and romance.

Alternative: Three pounds of strawberries may be substituted for the cherries, yielding a marvelous wine with similar magickal results. However, please note that strawberries are *very* active fermenters and extra caution will have to be taken with excess pressure in your aging containers.

Plum Affectionate

1 gal. spring water	15 good size plums
1 strand saffron	3 lbs. sugar
1 tsp. rose water	1/3 pkg. sparkling yeast

Directions: Bring your water to a low rolling boil while plums are being sliced and all pits are removed. Please note that your fruit should be sweet and ripe. The plums need to simmer in the water for a half hour until the liquid turns very red. Now add your sugar, saffron, and rose water, following the basic recipe for wine. Watch your wine closely. When it begins to get tart, return the entire batch to the stove, adding more plums and sugar until the taste is slightly sweeter than you might like. Age again, and repeat this process one more time for an almost liqueur-like wine.

At this point, sweeten to personal taste, boil, strain, and rebottle for gift giving or your own enjoyment.

Magickal Associations: Long life, kinship, companionship, and sexual compatibility.

History/Lore: In Eastern lands, plums are regarded as an emblem of friendship. It also represents immortality, because it is the first tree to begin to show signs of life in Spring.

Pineapple Passion for 2

1 1/2 cups pineapple juice   1 1/2 cups passion fruit juice
1/2 cup crushed pineapple   2 tsp. sweetener syrup
1 tsp. vanilla extract   dash cinnamon

Directions: Place all ingredients in a blender and whip up the passion!

Magickal Associations: Desire, attractiveness, affection.

History/Lore: Just by its name, passion fruit elicits certain expectations. Pineapple is the balancing point to this recipe, allowing our desires to be centered on one special individual.

Alternative: For even more sensual vigor, try using blackberry or mango juice instead of the pineapple.

Cafe Exhilaration

3 cups banana-flavored coffee   1/2 tsp. cinnamon
1 tsp. vanilla   1 cup heavy cream
1/2 ripe banana   sugar to taste
5 ice cubes

Directions: This is a marvelously easy beverage to prepare. Place all your ingredients in the blender, except for the ice, and whip until thick and frothy. Then add ice and chop finely so that the consistency is like a frappe. Garnish with a cherry!

Magickal Associations: Conception, fertility, sexual pleasure, and prowess.

History/Lore: Banana is used in this beverage to encourage sexual potency, while vanilla and cinnamon are used to improve desire.

SUN AND MOON

"That orbed continent, the fire that severs day from night"
—Shakespeare

The Sun in the morning and the Moon at night: These are two images on which even the earliest humans felt they could depend. At first both were conferred with indwelling spirits, even to the point of each becoming a god or goddess in their own right. Later, people still associated the Sun and Moon with sacred powers, but also with specific magickal influences that affected life on Earth in various ways.

Throughout this book I've talked about using the Moon's phases and/or sunlight to energize your beverage efforts. Beyond that, however, what about creating beverages to emphasize the solar or lunar attributes you most need, or for special Sun and Moon celebrations? The key is knowing which items are considered hot/fiery and cold/watery. Here is a list to which you can refer:

Solar Components

bay	carnelian	chamomile
chrysanthemum	cinnamon	ginseng
lime	marigold	orange
pineapple	rice milk	rosemary
tea	walnut flavoring	grapefruit
distilled beverages	honey	red wine
saffron	tangerine	

For crystal tinctures, use amber, carnelian, tiger's eye, or topaz. Prepare these beverages in sunlight: at noon for the greatest potency, at dawn for hope, and at dusk for completion or endings. Serve in yellow or gold-tone cups.

Sunset Ale

1 1/2 lbs. malt extract
4 oz. crystal malt
1/2 tsp. gypsum
1/4 tsp. salt
1/4 cup dextrose

1/2 oz. bullion hops
1/8 oz. cascade pellets
1 gal. water
1/2 pkg. top fermenting
beer yeast

Directions: Bring your water to a low rolling boil, adding gypsum and salt. Now add malts and boil for 20 minutes. Remove a quarter cup of the liquid and cool to lukewarm in order to suspend the yeast in. Meanwhile, add the aromatic hops, simmering for 15 minutes (cascade) and cool. In a large container, place a half gallon of cold water with yeast. Pour the liquid into this and cover loosely. Watch for all signs of fermentation to cease, then add dextrose and age for four to six weeks, using a fermentation lock before bottling.

Magickal Associations: Fire and Sun magick, courage, vitality.

History/Lore: This ale, when properly made, has a color similar to amber, which was once thought to be the solidified essence of the setting sun's tears.

Alternatives: For a less bitter ale, eliminate Bullion hops.

Currant-Raspberry Delight

3 cups freshly picked
  (red or black)
3 cups water
6 cups Absolut Kurant

1 lb. frozen or fresh currants
  raspberries (red)
1 1/2 cups sugar (or to taste)

Directions: Place raspberries and currants together in a pan with water. Simmer over a low flame for two hours, pressing frequently with the back of a spoon. Remove and strain, keeping the fruit for tarts, ice cream topping, etc.

Place the juice back on the stove, slowly adding sugar. Taste frequently, making sure to add a little more than you like because this sweetness will be toned down considerably when you blend in the vodka. Bottle and age for one month.

Magickal Associations: Sun and Fire magicks (note the deep red color achieved in the finished product). If it comes out pink, it might be more appropriate for friendship and improved attitudes.

History/Lore: Currants were sometimes imported to England via Portugal along with oranges to benefit the Elizabethan table, where they quickly became favored for all manner of sweets, including jellies, comfits, and sotelties.

Alternative: For a smooth, older version of this beverage, use honey instead of sugar, and add more Fire herbs like cinnamon and ginger during simmering.

Fruit Salad

2 peaches	1/2 cup apricots
2 kiwi fruit	1/2 cup strawberries
1/2 cup raspberries	1 banana
1 cup skim milk or seltzer water	1 cup vanilla yogurt
1 whole cherry (garnish)	

Directions: Juice together the first six ingredients, then add the liquid to the milk and yogurt, garnishing with a cherry.

Magickal Associations: Abundance of energy, joy, productivity, and love. A good celebratory beverage for Summer rituals.

History/Lore: Apricots had their origins in Asia, where they were known as "sun eggs" because of their rich golden color. This magickally allows them to become an active energy source for your beverage, on which the symbolism of the other fruits is conveyed like bright beams of sunlight through your body.

Lunar Components

cabbage	coconut	cucumber
grape	lemon	lettuce
papaya	potato	blueberry
wintergreen	egg	melon
milk	passion fruit	white wine
yogurt		

For crystal tinctures, use beryl, moonstone, mother-of-pearl, or selenite. Prepare these beverages in moonlight: a full moon for fulfillment, a waxing moon for growth and progress, and a waning moon for decrease and banishing. Serve in white or silver cups.

Lemon Iced Tea

4 lemon tea bags
1 qt. boiling water
1 cup sugar

1/2 cup orange liqueur
1/2 cup raspberry liqueur
2 cups soda water

Directions: Steep the tea bags in boiling water and dissolve the sugar, allowing it to sit for 10 minutes before removing. Amount of sugar may be decreased for personal taste. Chill the tea, adding it cold to the liqueurs and soda (both likewise chilled). Pour this over ice, garnished with a lemon wedge. This beverage has a flavor similar to rainbow sherbet.

Magickal Associations: Positive experiences in relationships, especially new romance. Moon magick.

History/Lore: Lemons appearing in dreams, especially for women, portend good luck in romance and possibly love soon to follow.

Alternatives: Try dry champagne in place of soda water on celebratory occasions.

Maternity Cordial

1 tsp. anise
1 tsp. mugwort
1 cup hot water
1 cup white grape juice

1 Tbsp. borage flowers
1 Tbsp. raspberry leaves
2 tsp. ginseng
1 cup peach brandy

Directions: Place your herbs in a tea ball and allow them to steep in the hot water for 20 minutes. Chill this water, then add grape juice and brandy over ice.

Magickal Associations: Maternal instincts, Moon magick, Goddess energy, productivity.

History/Lore: Based on an idea presented in a recipe from the 1700s, this beverage not only encourages feminine fertility, but also the general spirit of motherhood to nurture, care for, and protect those we love.

Lunar Enchantment

1 pt. strawberries	1/2 musk melon
1/2 honey dew melon	1/2 orange
1 cup coconut milk	honey to taste

Directions: Follow general directions for juicing, adding the coconut milk last.

Magickal Associations: All lunar and Goddess magicks, especially those for completion of any creative project.

History/Lore: These round, watery fruits are under the ruling of the Moon and as such are perfect ingredients for beverages pertaining to artistic or imaginative endeavors.

VERSATILITY

"Important principles may and must be flexible"
—Abraham Lincoln

Some say the word *Wicca* developed indirectly from the willow tree, whose flexible bows bend easily against the winds of change, but do not break. The nature of our craft is to bend and redirect energy. In the process of doing this we also need to learn how to be flexible people whose spiritual expressions change with our own growth and transformations in the world around us.

Human beings, however, are very prone to habit. We like to cut out a niche and stay in that comfortable abode. We like life's road to be straight, smooth, and pothole free. Unfortunately, the path to magick and spiritual wholeness is rarely any of those things. This means Witches must be ready to modify their life and their arts so that magick doesn't stagnate and die. Versatility beverages are designed to help us do just that.

Basil, willow bark, and catnip are three herbs that seem to ease us into changes, as do strong lunar components such as grapefruit, melon, and grape. More important than the ingredients, however, is the manner in which you make these beverages. Use a blender, a microwave, or food processor as each of these utensils is noted for its transformational quality. The energy of your chosen kitchen tool then will saturate your ingredients, which should have been carefully chosen for the type of changes you're undergoing.

If you wish to try a crystal tincture, I recommend amber.

Flexibility Font

1 gal. water	3 lbs. fresh beets
5 oranges	5 inches gingerroot
5 cups sugar	1/2 pkg. wine yeast

Directions: Remove tops and roots of the beets, then chop the remainder, placing them in a large pot with the water. Bring to a low rolling boil, continuing to cook until tender (approximately 40 minutes). Reduce heat to simmer, adding orange peel, bruised and diced gingerroot, and the juice from the oranges. Let this mixture steep for 15 minutes, then add sugar stirring until dissolved. Cool until lukewarm and add yeast, which has been suspended in one-quarter cup warm water. Place in a large container for initial fermentation, using a balloon or fermentation lock, and watching for all signs of fermentation to cease. At this time taste your beverage and sweeten if necessary. Put the mixture into a fresh jug, leaving any sediment in the bottom of the old container. Allow to age for another two months before bottling.

Magickal Associations: Versatility, adaptability, and awareness, especially in interpersonal relationships.

History/Lore: A wine similar to this is sometimes used in the Jewish Passover observances. Beet juice is considered an appropriate magickal alternative to blood and is strongly associated with human emotions, especially love. Five is used repeatedly in this recipe to encourage the energy of insight.

Coffee Adaptation

8 oz. milk

1/4 tsp. vanilla extract

1 tsp. instant coffee dissolved in 1 tsp. water

2 Tbsp. heavy cream

1 Tbsp. sugar

1/4 tsp. butterscotch flavoring

Directions: Beat the heavy cream to peaking and put in a large glass. Separately, blend your other ingredients until bubbly, then pour over cream. This may also be prepared warm.

Magickal Associations: Energy, vigor, initiative, and stamina that will help you move with the flow, rather than lag behind it.

History/Lore: Coffee beans originally were made into wine by African nations, not the hot beverage we know today. It was not until nearly 1000 C.E. when Arabs considered this alternative. The stimulating effect quickly became popular and also gives us its natural magickal associations.

Heartening Hawthorn

2 cups hawthorn flowers

1 ltr. peach juice

1 slice lemon

sugar or honey to taste

2 cups water

1 tsp. almond extract

1 slice orange

Directions: Place hawthorn flowers in warm water and allow to steep for 30 minutes. Strain and pour this liquid into a larger pan with remaining ingredients. Warm over low flame, adding sugar or honey until desired sweetness is acquired. Serve over ice chips with slivered almonds as garnish.

Magickal Associations: Revising goals using reason and instinct as helpmates.

History/Lore: Known as the "flower of hope," hawthorn symbolized fertility and marriage in ancient Greece and Rome.

Hawthorn was a favorite flower to adorn May Poles and is part of the sacred Fairy tree trinity of Europe, the other two being oak and ash.

Tea Tonic

1/4 cup Paraguay tea (mate)	1 tsp. chamomile
1/8 cup rose-hips	1 qt. boiling water
1 slice lemon	honey or sugar

Directions: Prepare as you would any tea, using a tea ball or cloth bag for the loose chamomile and rose hips. Lemon and sugar are added in the cup per personal tastes.

Magickal Associations: Adjusting to erratic energies, centering, and balance.

History/Lore: This beverage, besides having magickal restorative features, is rich in caffeine, vitamins, and physically rejuvenating qualities.

VICTORY AND SUCCESS

"The surest way not to fail is to determine to succeed."

—Richard Sheridan

Our society is very goal oriented, and even in our spiritual studies we find ourselves ever striving for the elusive "brass ring." There's really nothing wrong with that, so long as we've built solid foundations upon which to stand as we stretch our reach. However, even more than that, victory and success are heavily dependent on our self-confidence and faith. Without these two things, very little can be achieved mundanely or magickally.

The beverages in this section, therefore, are aimed at internalizing the confidence and faith necessary to bring about success, with a little luck and fortune tossed in for good measure.

The components commonly associated with these two goals are:

bay	chamomile	grapes
radish	rosemary	nasturtium
lemon balm	cinnamon	ginger

Success seems to center around the sun, so you may wish to make these beverages during the daylight hours. For crystal tinctures use amazonite, malachite, bloodstone, agate, or amber.

Parsley Triumph

1 qt. pineapple sage leaves	1/2 lb. parsley
1 gal. water	1 lemon
1 orange	3 lbs. orange blossom honey
1/2 pkg. yeast	

Directions: Place the herbs in a large crock. Bring the water to a full boil, then pour it over top the sage and parsley, allowing it to sit for a full 24 hours before straining. Squeeze to express any liquid from the herbs, then rewarm the herb water with the sliced fruit and honey until mixed well. Continue warming for 20 minutes, then allow to cool, straining off the fruit just before the addition of yeast. Proceed as in the basic recipe for wine.

Magickal Associations: Protection in new endeavors, preserving prosperity, accomplishment, success, and overcoming obstacles.

History/Lore: In both Greece and Rome, parsley was a symbol of victory and success. The plant itself was fabled to grow from the blood of an ancient fallen hero named Archemorus.

Gingered Glory

1 cup room temperature carbonated soda	2 pieces candied gingerroot
	1 lemon balm leaf
dash of cinnamon (optional)	

Directions: Follow general directions for soda pop, except place this mixture in an airtight container for about an hour before serving over ice for best flavor. If time is short, use some sweetener and ginger extract instead.

Magickal Associations: Sweet success, victory, positive culmination of efforts.

History/Lore Ginger is considered an herb, which accentuates energy towards specific goals. The additional benefit of this beverage is that it also tends to settle the stomach, allowing you to really focus on your magickal rites.

Alternative: For success specifically in areas of personal aspirations, add some expressed pomegranate juice to this mixture. About two tablespoons is good.

Achievement Beer

3" piece fresh gingerroot
1/4 cup Northern Brewer
   Hops (if available)
4 qts. hot water

1 lemon, peeled (retain) and
   juiced (retain)
1 1/2 cups sugar
1/4 oz. suspended beer yeast

Directions: Mince and crush the ginger with the flat back of a spoon or mortar and pestle. Put this in a large bowl with sugar and lemon peel, pouring the boiling water over top. Stir in hops and allow to steep until lukewarm. Now add lemon juice and yeast mixture. Cover the entire bowl and allow to sit for at least 12 hours before straining and bottling. Ready within five days, this beer retains good flavor for about a month.

Magickal Associations: Power, success, and victory.

History/Lore: Ginger was a widely known spice to the ancient world, being written about by Confucius and being eaten readily in cookies as early as the Egyptians in Cheops. This particular recipe, however, comes from the American frontier days.

Alternatives: When you add the boiling water, also consider adding various fruits to this mixture that reflect your goal. For example, strawberries might be included for a successful relationship.

Sparkling Success

1 cup orange pekoe tea	1 Tbsp. honey
1 cup orange juice	1 cup ginger ale
3 strawberries (garnish)	1 slice of orange (garnish)

Directions: Pre-prepare the orange tea (or orange spice). While it is still warm, stir in honey to dissolve. Cool, then blend together with orange juice and ginger ale. Serve chilled or over crushed ice with sliced strawberries and oranges for a bright, invigorating drink.

Magickal Associations: Maintaining the energy, vitality, and stamina necessary to reach your goals.

History/Lore: Tea has long been considered not only a social drink, but one that helps calm and relax. By adding to this the orange juice, noted for its healthful effects, and a little soda for "energy bubbles," this becomes a wonderful magick tonic when you need a pick-me-up.

Conqueror's Cup

1/2 handful of fresh woodruff	3 cups cider or apple juice
1 slice of orange	2 to 3 whole strawberries
2 tsp. sugar	

Directions: Rinse the woodruff and strawberries thoroughly. Place your ingredients together in a bowl and mix well. To increase the flavor, warm the cider or juice first. Chill the bowl for a minimum of one hour before straining and pouring into a large glass to enjoy. Garnish with the berries. A great springtime refresher!

Magickal Associations: Success, prosperity, protection, especially in "battles."

History/Lore: The beautiful white woodruff blossoms are considered sacred to the Goddess. In pre-Christian times, the bouquet of this flower was used predominantly to scent a variety of drinks. In the Middle Ages, woodruff was thought a good tonic for sickness, fever, and to purge the blood.

WISDOM

"Common sense in an uncommon degree is what the world calls wisdom."

—Samuel Taylor Coleridge

The path to enlightenment is filled with lessons aimed at improving our wisdom—wise choices, wise thoughts, wise actions, wise words. We mark our elders and teachers in the magickal community by their wisdom. Even so, it's not always an easy commodity to develop.

The beverages in this section are designed to help us integrate the energies necessary to begin living with wisdom as an ally. The ingredients for sagacity include:

almond	blue beverages	purple beverages
sage	mulberries	peach
honey	hazelnut	

Drink these brews from a golden cup, in the presence of sunlight, which banishes the shadows of uncertainty. For crystal elixirs use jade or sodalite.

Sage's Beer

8 cups hot ale	1 1/2 tsp. nutmeg
1 1/2 tsp. gingerroot, ground	brown sugar to taste
8 baked apples, peeled and cored	

Directions: Pulp the apple pith and brown sugar together until you like the flavor that results. Add to this nutmeg and ginger. Now, slowly add the warmed ale, stirring until well blended. If desired, float some sweet cakes on top.

Magickal Associations: Earth magicks, the harvest, wisdom.

History/Lore: Known sometimes by English countrymen as Lambs Wool, this drink was often prepared on the first day of August to honor the angel who protects fruits, seeds, and all that grows from the land. One cannot help but notice the similarity of this term to "Lamas" or "La mas ubal," which literally translates to "day of the apple." The number eight is used in this recipe as a number for personal change, improved control, and the fulfillment of acumen.

Apple-Almond Erudition

1 gal. peach juice	2 oz. sliced almonds
1 Tbsp. almond extract	2 lbs. honey
1/2 pkg. yeast	1 cup almond or peach liqueur
1 ltr. vodka or white rum	

Directions: Warm the peach juice with the almonds over a low flame for 20 minutes. Add honey, turning up the heat to boil for 15 minutes, skimming all the while. Cool and add almond extract. Add yeast and allow to sit in the open air for 24 hours before straining into fermentation vessel. This will need a balloon or lock to clarify for two months before siphoning off and adding spirits. Age another year.

Magickal Associations: Sagacity.

History/Lore: Eating almonds inspires wisdom, as do peaches. The additional benefit to the peach juice here is that it can help you wisely obtain your desires. Make a wish before you drink it!

Clarification Cup

1 cup apple juice wisdom	1 tsp. lemon juice
1 tsp. honey	cinnamon stick
1 cherry	1 egg white, beaten

Directions: Warm the apple juice just to the point of almost boiling, then add lemon and honey, which are stirred with the cinnamon stick. Place egg white over the top of the drink with a cherry in the middle (sundae style)!

History/Lore: The apple juice brings wisdom balanced against lemon's cleansing clarity. The entire hot beverage is immersed in snow, with the cherry on the top to help improve personal focus and balance. Visualize this in the middle of your gravity center.

Peachy Keen Punch

1 qt. peach juice   1 tsp. rum extract
1 cup sugar   1 lemon, juiced
1 lemon, thinly sliced

Directions: Mix the first four ingredients in a blender before pouring into the punch bowl. For a frothy top, add one egg white. Float lemon slices on top as garnish.

Magickal Associations: Sagacity, good judgment, and prudence.

History/Lore: The peach is a fruit of wisdom and its pit (the core of growth) is a good addition to medicine bags.

Alternatives: If you have a group who has a particularly difficult time with funding, add pineapple juice or chunks to this punch to encourage wisdom in spending.

Spiced Lemon

1 gal. boiling water   1" bruised ginger
1 stick cinnamon   4 to 5 whole cloves
4 to 5 allspice beads   1/2 tsp. cream of tartar
1 lb. sugar   2 lemon peels grated
1/2 cup hop flowers   juice of two lemons
1/4 pkg. active yeast

Directions: Place the first nine ingredients together in your brewing pan and boil vigorously for 15 minutes. Strain and cool, adding the juice from the two lemons previously peeled and yeast, suspended in warm water. This needs to sit for 24 hours uncovered (or put some cheese cloth on top the pan to keep dust out). Strain and bottle. Ready to drink in 5 to 7 days.

Magickal Associations: Wisdom, caution, clarity, prudence.

History/Lore: In the language of flowers, the lemon is a sign of discretion, tolerance, and forbearance. Its tangy flavor helps to bring lucidity and precision to mental functions.

Alternative: To further accent the cognitive energy of this beverage, add two teaspoons of rosemary with the other herbs. This beverage also makes a super marinade for chicken.

Snow Song

2 cups pear juice   1 slice of lemon
1 egg white, beaten

Directions: Pour pear juice into a large glass. Squeeze lemon slice into the juice with one heaping teaspoon of beaten egg white and stir. Place remaining egg white on top to look like peaks of snow.

Magickal Associations: Clarity of thought.

History/Lore: Not only does this beverage have a pale white glimmer of snow, but the lemon adds precision to our contemplative processes. Additionally, this beverage can improve your focus in an emotional situation.

Alternatives: To improve wisdom with regard to spiritual insights, add fresh or juiced peaches to this recipe.

BEVERAGES, INGREDIENTS, AND DIVINE/MAGICKAL ASSOCIATIONS

"He (Osiris) also invented the beverage made from barley called beer, and which in taste and flavor is not much inferior to wine. He taught its preparation to those whose country is unsuited for the cultivation of the vine."

—Diodor Sic., IV.2

Those readers wishing to make beverages to use as offerings, libations, and/or for serving at thematic celebrations will find this appendix very helpful. Here you can review various ingredients for their elemental associations, common magickal applications, and deities to whom they were considered sacred. From there it isn't too hard to design a brew suited to your needs, the ritual's focus, and/or the sacred power being venerated.

To illustrate: The festival of Summer solstice is best observed with Fire-oriented beverages, because it celebrates the power of light over darkness. In this case, one might create a beer to which cinnamon or another "Fire" herb has been added. This beverage would also be suited to several Egyptian deities, including Isis. As a libation, it would work very effectively to increase power and protection in the sacred circle. There's nothing that says you can't multitask your beverages! In fact, I encourage it.

In reviewing this list, bear in mind it is very abbreviated and limited to edible items. It would take an entire book to cover all the magickal, spiritual, and religious symbolism behind all the potential ingredients for your brews. Consequently, I highly recommend getting a couple of metaphysical herb or food books to act as backup resources. In particular, Paul Beyerl's *Herbal Magick*, Scott Cunningham's *Magick in Food*, and my *Magick Made Easy* are all good reference, to which you can turn again and again in your mystical arts.

Ale or Beer: Elementally Fire. Used regularly for offerings and purification. Sacred to Tenemit, Isis, and Hathor in Egypt, Shoney in Scotland, and Kremana in Slavonic regions.

Allspice: Elementally Fire. An herb of luck, prosperity, health, and productive imagining.

Almond: Elementally Air. Magickally attuned to money matters, devotion, love, and self-sufficiency. Sacred to Artemis, Cybele, Hecate, and Zeus in Greece, Ptah in Egypt, and Chandra in India.

Anise: Elementally Air. An herb of energy, purification, and blessing. Sacred to Apollo, Mercury, and Hermes (Greco-Roman).

Apple: Elementally Water. Apple juice provides discernment, health, prudence, love, and inner vision. Sacred to numerous deities including Induna and Odin (Norse), Venus and Apollo (Rome), and Zeus and Hera (Greece).

Banana: Elementally Air. Banana promotes male sexuality, devotion, and safety. Also an appropriate flavoring for Summerland (death) rituals. Sacred to Kanaloa (Hawaii).

Basil: Elementally Fire. Use this for house blessing libations, initiatory beverages, purification, and courage. Sacred to Krishna and Vishnu (India).

Bay: Elementally Fire. An herb of vitality, protection, success, and power. Whole bay leaves can promote these energies just as garnishes. Sacred to Eros, Apollo, and Adonis (Greece), Buddha (India), and Fides (Rome).

Blackberry: Elementally Water. Use this for magickal healing beverages. A suitable offering for Venus (Rome).

Caraway: Elementally Air. Used extensively in love and devotion potions, as well as an herb that promotes Earth-healing. Suited as a flavoring for post-harvest celebratory feasts where it promotes wisdom with our resources.

Carrot: Elementally Fire. Carrot juice encourages a deep connection with the sensual/sexual self, especially in men. Also helps ground out excess energy and promote insight. It is not associated with a deity that I could discern.

Catnip: Elementally Water. An herb of fertility, charm, playfulness, and instinct. Sacred to Bast (Egypt).

Celery: Elementally Fire (with strong Water undertones). Magickally used for mental clarity and to promote passion (thus the combination of Fire/Water). It was not associated with a deity that I could discern.

Chamomile: Elementally Fire. Use chamomile for any solar observance. It is also suited to garden libations, health, peacefulness, and new beginnings.

Cherry: Elementally Water. A fruit juice filled with psychic energy, love, and playfulness. An excellent choice for pathworking rituals where creativity and sensitivity are required. Many magickal practitioners feel cherry-flavored beverages are suitable for honoring the youthful Goddess.

Cinnamon: Elementally Fire. A good aromatic for strength and success. Sacred to Greco-Roman love goddesses like Aphrodite and Venus, which is the reason it was used as an aphrodisiac.

Clove: Elementally Fire. An herb of protection, prosperity, and kinship and love. If you have a Malaysian god or goddess that you follow, this is considered a suitable offering for him or her.

Coconut: Elementally Water. Excellent for lunar magick of any type. Sacred to the goddess Sri in India.

Coffee: Elementally Fire. Drink to stimulate the conscious mind, alertness, and for hospitality rituals.

Cranberry: Elementally Water (as juice) or Fire (in berry form due to color). A good protective juice that is sacred to Marjatta, a youthful Finish goddess. Ideal for Yule rituals.

Currant: Elementally Fire and Water. A fruit of abundance. Use red currants for Fire festivals and white ones for Winter rituals.

Daisy: Elementally Water. A flower that represents youth, simplicity, and future telling. Sacred to Freya (Germany).

Dandelion: Elementally Air. A flower attuned to wish magick, astral awareness, and divination. Sacred to Hecate and Theseus (Greece).

Dill: Elementally Fire. This herb protects from negative magick, encourages restfulness, friendship, and mental clarity. Excellent ingredient for unity/fellowship rituals.

Fennel: Elementally Fire. Suited to protection, physical health, and for banishing ill-intended magick. Sacred to Prometheus (Greek).

Fig: Elementally Fire. This fruit adds power, love, wisdom, enlightenment, and fecundity to beverages. Sacred to Ra and Isis (Egypt), Brahma (India) and Juno (Greece).

Garlic: Elementally Fire. Use garlic for protection, Fire magick, and when working with the goddess Hecate (Greek).

Ginger: Elementally Fire. An herb of victory, power, prosperity, and romance. A good ingredient for beverages and brews aimed at consecration.

Grain: Elementally Earth. Used mostly for beer or liquefied nutrition for invalids, grains are aligned with energy for luck, prosperity, and good health. Barley was sacred to Demeter (Greece) and Vishnu (India).

Grape: Elementally Water. The fruit of celebration, joy, and abundance. Sacred to Bacchus (Rome), Hathor (Egypt), and Iznagi (Japan).

Heather: Elementally Water. A flower found in wines, teas, and some meads, heather evokes good fortune, inner beauty, networking, and self-awareness. An excellent ingredient for rain libations, or invoking Isis (Egypt) and Venus (Rome).

Honey: Elementally Air. Honey purifies, attracts happiness, motivates fertility, inspires romance, and generally brings "sweetness" to the energy of your brews. Sacred to many deities including Min (Egypt), Ea (Babylon), Artemis (Greece), and Kama (India).

Kiwi: Elementally Water. A fruit that fosters hopeful, innocent love and a sense of relaxation. A good addition to Summer beverages.

Lavender: Elementally Air. This herb brings inner peace, decreases stress, and promotes joy. Often used for wedding rituals and to invoke Saturn.

Lemon: Elementally Water. Lemon juice bears the energy of purification, refreshment, unity, and longevity. Sacred to the Buddhist deity Jambhala.

Lime: Elementally Water. Use lime juice to attract the Fairy folk and devas, especially those that abide in the stones and soil.

Mango: Elementally Fire. Use mango juice to inspire romance and love. Sacred to Buddha.

Marigold: Elementally Fire. Use this in beverages for Fire, solar festivals, or summerland rituals, and as an ingredient that accents love, peace, inner vision, consecration, and truthfulness. Sacred to Mary in Christianity.

Marjoram: Elementally Air. An herb of happiness, bounty, health, and overall well-being. Sacred to Venus (Rome) and therefore quite suited to marriage rituals.

Milk: Elementally Water. Attuned to the Goddess aspect, maternal instincts, and lunar energy. Sacred to Hathor and Isis (Egypt), and Zeus (Greek), among others.

Mint: Elementally Air. An herb of blessing, success, prosperity, revitalization, and passion. Sacred to Pluto (Rome).

Mulberry: Elementally Air. This fruit juice bears wisdom, practicality, psychism, and inventiveness to the drinker. Sacred to Minerva (Rome).

Nutmeg: Elementally Fire. Nutmeg brings good fortune, fidelity, and well-being. Sacred to many Indian gods and goddesses.

Orange: Elementally Fire. Orange provides us with love, luck, prosperity, health, and devotion. Sacred to Apollo and Hera (Greece). Because of its tropical nature and color, a good solar symbol and recommended juice for Sun festivals.

Passion Fruit: Elementally Water. This fruit inspires exactly what you'd expect from its name: romance and passion. It can also promote friendship and peace.

Peach: Elementally Water. Peaches bear the energies of longevity, good wishes, protection, wisdom, and fertility. Sacred to Hai Wang Ma (China) and Iznagi (Shinto).

Pear: Elementally Water. A good fruit for magickal lust, zeal, and enthusiasm. Sacred to Athena (Greece).

Pineapple: Elementally Fire. This promotes good fortune, prosperity, dedication, safety, hospitality, and follow-through. It is also a good cleanser.

Plum: Elementally Water. Plums provide energy for adoration, respect, and protection. A suitable juice or wine to use in offerings to Japanese gods and goddesses.

Pomegranate: Elementally Fire. This fruit manifests creative vision, inventiveness, and prosperity. It is also a blood substitute for old spells that call for it. Sacred to Dionysus and Persephone (Greece), and Ceres (Rome), among others.

Potato: Elementally Earth. Use this vegetable to ground out excess energy, for Earth-centered magicks, and to promote health. Sacred to the Potato Mother (Peru).

Quince: Elementally Earth. Good for beverages aimed at happiness, safety, and personal fulfillment. Sacred to Venus (Rome).

Raspberry: Elementally Water. Use this to encourage love, protection, happiness, and abundance. Figuratively also a good juice when you want to shake off negative influences (e.g. giving them the "raspberry").

Rhubarb: Elementally Earth. This encourages protection, faithfulness, devotion, and well-being.

Rice Milk: Elementally Air. Rice has amuletic qualities and boosts the fertile energy of a beverage. Sacred to the goddess Ukemochi (Shinto).

Rose: Elementally Water. The pinnacle of love potions, and a nice addition to those for health, divination, intuition, and sensual awareness. Sacred to Venus (Rome) and Aphrodite (Greece).

Rosemary: Elementally Fire. Memory retention, the conscious mind, purification, responsibility, fidelity, and youthful energy are found in this herb. Sacred to Venus (Rome) and Mary in Christianity.

Saffron: Elementally Fire. Excellent herb for solar observances. Also attuned to magick for weather changes, prosperity, joy, psychism, leadership, and passion. Sacred to Eos (Greece), Amon Ra (Egypt), and Brahma (Hindu).

Sage: Elementally Air. An herb of wisdom, mental wellness, decision-making, health, and good business sense. Sacred to Cornus (Rome) and Zeus (Greece).

Strawberry: Elementally Water. Use strawberries to emphasize happiness, love, and a youthful outlook. An excellent flavoring for Lammas rituals. Sacred to Freya (Norse/Teutonic).

Sugar: Elementally Earth. A key ingredient to improve negative dispositions. Also a good offering for ancestral spirits.

Tea: Elementally Fire and Water. Tea brings prosperity, courage, strength, vitality, health, and inner peace. A suitable offering for many Chinese and Japanese deities.

Thyme: Elementally Water. Use thyme to motivate bravery, fortitude, cleansing, awareness, and as a gardening libation. A suitable offering for fairies and devas.

Vanilla: Elementally Water. Vanilla bean or pure flavoring is magickally geared toward productivity, energy, mental awareness, and love.

Watermelon: Elementally Water. Add this to beverages for love, health, and fertility. Sacred to Set (Egypt).

Wine: Elementally Fire with Water undertones. An excellent offering for many divine beings. Wine has an overall upbeat energy, promoting happiness. Sacred to Gestin (Sumeria), Ishtar (Mesopotamia), Osiris and Isis (Egypt), and Bacchus (Rome).

Yogurt: Elementally Water. Use this to emphasize spirituality, awareness, and health.

SYMBOLISM AND CORRESPONDENCES

Symbolism is very important to magick. It gives sensual forms to our desires and improves our overall focus. It also provides very real emotional connections to the process, which in turn increases manifesting energy. You may want to use some of these ideas in preparing your own witchy beverages and brews, so here are some correspondence lists to which to refer.

COLOR CORRESPONDENCES

Choose your ingredients' colors so they represent the goal of the magick. Note: It need not be just one color—you can blend hues to likewise blend energies. Also, if you can't find ingredients of the correct color, don't overlook food coloring!

Blue	Peace, joy, tranquility, the Water element.
Brown	Grounding, foundations, the Earth element.
Orange	Friendship, warmth, and productivity.
Green	Growth, healing, hope (alternative Earth element).
Purple	Spirituality, leadership, and wisdom.
Red	Vitality, energy, passion, the Fire element.
White	Purity, spirit, Goddess magick.
Yellow	Communication, creativity, God magick, the Air element.

Number Correspondences

There are three very easy ways to use numeric symbolism in your potions. First is by having a set number of ingredients. This is a really nice option when you don't have components that adequately represent your goal. Here, the number becomes your symbolic value on which to focus.

The second option is stirring the blend a set number of times. Move clockwise for positive, growing energy and counter clockwise for banishing or diminishing energies. If this number is not sufficient for blending your brew, you have two options. First you can use a larger number that breaks down to your desired number through numerological reduction. For example: 21 = 2+1 = 3. The other option is to mix up the beverage completely and then add an incantation, visualization, or other magickal method on the last few stirs.

Finally, if you're making beer, wine, or other aged beverages, you can time the preparation so that the number of days, weeks, months, or years that you age it is significant. For example, a beverage being served at initiation might be aged for a year and a day—the traditional amount of time a novice studies before taking this step.

Symbolism

1	Singularity, beginnings, the Sun, and the self.
2	Duality, alternatives, partnerships.
3	Body-mind-spirit connection, fortitude, symmetry.
4	The Earth element, success, achievement, foundations.
5	Insight, adaptability, flexibility.
6	Determination, completion, protection.
7	Diversity, awareness, the Moon.
8	Wholeness, leadership, change, power.
9	Universal truths.
10	Fulfillment, the conscious/logical mind.
12	Cycles, endurance.
13	Certainty, devotion, abundance.

TIMING CORRESPONDENCES

Most people use the Moon's cycles, if they're schedules allow, in brewing up magickal beverages. This is the easiest celestial object to track, as its phases are often put on even mundane calendars these days! While it is certainly not necessary to use timing as an additional dimension to your witchy efforts, it can help when other factors are lacking (like the right ingredients).

Dark Moon	Focus on brews for banishing negativity, those intended to bring rest, or those that will be applied to weed out old habits or ideas.
Waxing Moon	Considered the best time to make alcoholic beverages for pleasing results. Magickally attuned to growth, progress, improvements, and generating positive energy.
Full Moon	Completion and fulfillment are in this phase, along with plenty of power for manifestation. Also an excellent time to make goddess-oriented beverages, or those for psychic endeavors.
Waning	A phase that symbolizes slow reduction or disappearance. If there's something you want to "phase out" of your life, this is an ideal time to try your magick.
Blue Moon	Miracles—expect anything!

If you find you have trouble using moon phases, try seasons or holidays instead. For example, any harvest festival like Thanksgiving is a good time to work with apple juice and other harvest-related fruit/vegetable juices. Autumn also accentuates the ability to "harvest" whatever energies you've sown earlier in the year. Similarly, on May Day—a traditional Fire festival—make a beverage that's filled with fiery herbs or fruits to honor the day.

POSSIBLE BREWING DEITIES

"These things surely lie on the knees of the gods"
—Homer

Reading the myths and legends of many cultures is an enriching experience. In the process, you get a clearer understanding of how diverse our world has been throughout history, and insight into why we are as well as who we are. Among these legends, many Divine images appear, and reappear, inspiring humanity towards better living.

Earlier in this book, I briefly mentioned calling on a Divine presence to bless magickal-brewing efforts. The obvious question for most Wiccans and Pagans is which visage of god/goddess to choose? Ultimately, we could look to one which rules over a specific attribute or element, such as Thor for weather-related beverages used in libations, or Athena for elixirs of romance. Beyond this, we can also consider the gods and goddesses who have somehow been associated with a specific beverage, fruit, spice, vegetable, or grain according to our chosen ingredients (see also Appendix A).

Either of these approaches is perfectly good. Just decide which one makes the most sense to, and works the best for, you. Also weigh the possibility of calling on two or more gods and goddesses; one who can sanctify the metaphysical goals of your brew, and another to consecrate the components. This approach is nice because it affords an improved spiritual balance in your work environment and the final product.

Besides those provided in Appendix A, below are some possible gods, goddesses, heroes, heroines, and even saints to choose from, including their country of origin and spheres of influence. This list could be *much* longer, but I have limited myself to some of the more interesting and assorted options here. For additional ideas, look at fruits or spices sacred to your patron Deities and check resource books like *The Witches God, The Witches Goddess* (Janet & Stewart Farrar) and *Ancient Shining Ones* (DJ Conway).

Apollo: Greek; as a god of science, music, and poetry, Apollo is sometimes associated with mead. His "science" aspect combined with art make him a good choice to call on to hone your skills in general brewing efforts.

Ahurani: Persian; goddess of water.

Anat: Canaanite; fertility goddess who is appropriate for any milk-based beverage.

Aphrodite: Greek; goddess of love. Any beverage with roses, clover, sweet aromas, or apples.

Athena: Greek; warrior goddess. Any beverage with coconut. In Rome known as Minerva.

Baldur: Norse; god of sacred wells and light. Good for non-alcoholic beverages that are going to be used for magick.

Binah: Hebrew; the supernatural Mother also known as "she who nourishes." Her cabalistic symbol is the cup.

Blodeuwedd: Welsh; known as "flower face," any flower-based drinks, especially those with broom or meadowsweet.

Bragi: Norse; keeper of the mead of inspiration, god of eloquence and wisdom.

Buddhi: Tibetan; goddess of achievement. Ask for her aid in learning your art(s).

Carmenta: Roman; inventor of arts and sciences, similar in function to Buddhi.

Ceres: Roman; goddess of agriculture. Appropriate for most beverages, but beer especially.

Cerridwen: Welsh; goddess of the cauldron and grain.

Chicomecoatz: Aztec; goddess of maize and rural abundance; good for corn-based drinks and harvest festival beverages.

Cormus: Greek; god of laughter and mirth, good for celebratory brewing efforts.

Dionysus: Greek; god of wine and mead. In Rome known as Bacchus or Liber and has similar personifications in almost every culture.

Esculapius: Greek; god of physick and all health beverages.

Euphrosyne: Greek; muse who rejoices the heart.

Frigg: Norse; personification of Earth, especially appropriate for beverages of libation.

Gambrinus: Germanic; dubbed the inventor of beer and patron saint of beer and brewers in this country.

Ganemede: The cupbearer to Jupiter, good for hospitality.

Gibil: Babylonian; god of arbitration, especially good for beverages prepared for oath cups or peace cups.

A Witch's Beverages and Brews

Gunnloed: Teutonic; god of mead.

Hesperides: Greek; three sisters with golden apples in their magick garden.

Hygeia: Greek; goddess of health.

I: Chinese; god of archery who possesses the drink of immortality.

Idun: Norse; keeper of apples of immortality.

Isis: Egyptian; goddess whose sacred fruits include figs and dates and whose offerings often consisted of beer, milk, and wine.

Ivenopae: Indonesian; Mother of rice, good to bless saki. Also consider Inari from Japan or Gauri from India as alternatives.

Kanaloa: Hawaii; goddess whose sacred fruit is the banana.

Lares and **Penates:** Roman; home and hearth gods.

Momus: Greek; god of raillery.

Nikkal: Canaanite; goddess of first fruits, good for beverages to be used in offerings.

Oegir: Norse; beer brewer of Asgard.

Omacatl: Aztec; god of delight and celebration.

Osiris: Egyptian; god of cereals and common people, especially appropriate for beer.

Pomona: Roman; goddess of fruits and Autumn. All fruit-based beverages or harvest drinks.

Shoney: Scotland; god of ale. Mirrored in Egypt by Tenemit.

Thor: Norse; red fruited drinks.

Vertumnus: Roman; god of orchards.

Wang Mu: China; goddess who was served the peaches of immortality.

U.S. TO METRIC CONVERSION CHART

DRY MEASURE	
¼ cup	70 ml
⅓ cup	105 ml
½ cup	140 ml
¾ cup	210 ml
1 cup	275 ml
WEIGHT	
1 oz.	30 g
2 oz.	60 g
4 oz.	115 g
6 oz.	170 g
8 oz.	225 g
10 oz.	280 g
12 oz.	340 g
14 oz.	400 g
16 oz.	450 g

LIQUID MEASURE	
1 oz.	30 ml
2 oz. / ¼ cup	60 ml
4 oz. / ½ cup	120 ml
6 oz. / ¾ cup	180 ml
8 oz. / 1 cup	235 ml
1 ½ cup	355 ml
16 oz. / 2 cups	475 ml
32 oz. / 4 cups	950 ml
64 oz. / 2 qt.	1.9 l
128 oz. / gallon	3.8 l
LENGTH	
¼ inch	6.5 mm
½ inch	13 mm
¾ inch	19 mm
1 inch	25 mm
TEMPERATURE	
(Fahrenheit minus 32 degrees; multiply the remainder by 5/9 = Celsius)	
200° Fahrenheit	93° Celsius
250° F	120° C
300° F	150 C
325° F	163° C
350° F	177° C
375° F	190° C
400° F	205° C
425° F	218° C
450° F	232° C

BIBLIOGRAPHY

Arnold, John P. *Origin and History of Beer and Brewing.* Chicago: Wahl-Henius Institute of Fermentology, 1911.

Aylett, Mary. *Country Wines.* London: Odhams, 1953.

Baker, Margaret. *Folklore & Customs of Rural England.* Totawa, NJ: Rowman & Littlefield, 1974.

Bartlett, John. *Familiar Quotations.* Boston: Little Brown & Co., 1938.

Belt, T. Edwin. *Vegetable, Herb & Cerial Wines.* London: Mills & Boon LTD, 1971.

_____. *Flower, Leaf & Sap Wines.* London: Mills & Boon LTD, 1971.

Beyerl, Paul. *Herbal Magick.* Custer, WA: Phoenix Publising, 1998.

Beyerl, Paul. *Master Book of Herbalism.* Custer, WA: Phoenix Publishing, 1984.

Black, William George. *Folk Medicine.* New York: Burt Franklin, 1883.

Broth, Patricia, and Don Broth. *Food in Antiquity.* New York: Frederick A. Praeger, 1969.

Chase, A. W. M.D. *Receipt Book & Household Physician.* Detroit, MI: F. B. Dickerson Company, 1908.

Chase, Edithe L., W. E. P. French. *Waes Hale.* New York: Grafton Press, 1903.

Chow, Kit, and Kramer Ione. *All the Tea in China.* San Francisco: China Books and Periodicals, 1990.

Clarkson, Rosetta. *Green Enchantment.* New York: McMillian Publishing, 1940.

Clifton, C. *Edible Flowers.* New York: McGraw-Hill, 1976.

Complete Anachronist Guide to Brewing. Milpitas, CA: Society for Creative Anactronsim, 1983.

Culpepper, Nicholas. *Complete Herbal and English Physician.* Glenwood, IL: Meyerbooks, 1991. Originally published 1841.

Cunningham, Scott. *Encyclopedia of Magical Herbs.* St. Paul, MN: Llewellyn Publications, 1988.

_____. *The Magic in Food.* St. Paul, MN: Llewellyn Publications, 1991.

_____. *The Magic of Incense, Oils and Brews.* St. Paul, MN: Llewellyn Publications, 1988.

Davids, Kenneth. *Coffee.* San Francisco: 101 Productions, 1976.

Digby, Kenelm. *The Closet Opened.* London: E.L.T. Brome, Little Britian, 1696.

Doorn, Joyce V. *Making your own Liquors.* San Leandro, CA: Prism Press, 1977.

Elspan, Ceres. *Herbs to Help you Sleep.* Boulder, CO: Shambhala Press, 1980.

Every Day Life through the Ages. London: Readers Digest Association, 1992.

Foster, Carol. *Cooking with Coffee.* New York: Fireside Books, 1992.

Fox, William M.D. *Family Botanic Guide,* 18th edition. Sheffield, England: William Fox and Sons, 1907.

Freeman, Margaret. *Herbs for the Medieval Household for cooking, Healing and Divers Uses.* New York: Metropolitan Museum of Art, 1943.

Freid, Mimi. *Liquors for Gifts.* Charlotte, VT: Garden Way Publishing, 1988.

French, R. K. *The History and Virtues of Cyder.* New York: St. Martin's Press, 1982.

Gayre, Robert. *Brewing Mead,* Boulder, CO: Brewers Publications, 1986.

Gordon, Lesley. *Green Magic.* New York: Viking Press, 1977.

Haggard, Howard W. M.D. *Mystery, Magic and Medicine.* Garden City, NY: Doubleday & Co., 1933.

Hale, William Harlan. *Horizon Cookbook & Illustrated History of Eating and Drinking.* Garden City, NY: Doubleday and Company, 1968.

Hall, Manly. *Secret Teachings of All Ages.* Los Angeles: Philosophical Research Society, 1977.

Hardwick, Homer. *Winemaking at Home.* New York: W. Funk, 1954.

Hechtlinger, Adelaide. *The Seasonal Hearth.* New York: Overlook Press, 1986.

Hiss, Emil. *Standard Manual of Soda & Other Beverages.* Chicago, IL: GP Englehand & Co, 1897.

Hobson, Phyllis. *Wine, Beer & Softdrinks.* Charlotte, VT: Garden Way Publishing.

Honey, Babs. *Drinks for All Seasons.* Wakefield, England: E.P. Publishing Ltd, 1982.

Hopkins, Albert A. *Home Made Beverages.* New York: Scientific American Publishing Company, 1919.

Hosletters US Almanac. Pittsburg, PA: Hosletter Co, 1897.

Hunter, Beatrice. *Fermented Foods and Beverages.* New Canaan, CT: Keats Publishing, 1973.

Hutchinson, Ruth, and Ruth Adams. *Every Day's a Holiday.* New York: Harper & Brothers, 1951.

Jagendorf, M. A.. *Folk Wines, Cordials & Brandies.* New York: Vanguard Press, 1963.

Kieckhefer, Richard. *Magic in the Middle Ages.* Melbourne, Australia: Cambridge University Press, 1989.

Long, Cheryl. *Classic Liqueurs.* Oswego, OR: Culinary Arts, 1990.

Lorie, Peter. *Superstitions.* New York: Simon & Schuster, 1992.

Lowe, Carl. *Juice Power.* New York: Berkley Books, 1992.

Luce, Henry R., editor. *Beverages.* Alexandria, VA: Time Life Books, 1982.

MacNicol, Mary. *Flower Cookery.* New York: Fleet Press, 1967.

Magnall, Richmal. *Historical and Miscellanious Questions.* London, England: Longman, Brown, Green and Longman, 1850.

Mares, William. *Making Beer.* New York: Alfred A. Knopf Co, 1992.

Marshall, Mac, ed., *Beliefs, Behaviors and Alcoholic Beverages.* Michigan: University of Michigan Press, 1979.

Murray, Keith. *Ancient Rites & Ceremonies.* Toronto, Canada: Tudor Press, 1980.

Murray, Michael T. *The Healing Power of Herbs.* Rocklin, CA: Prima Publishing, 1992.

Olney, Bruce. *Liqueurs, Aperitifs and Fortified Wines.* London, England: Mills & Boon LTD, 1972.

Opie, Iona and Moria Tatem. *Dictionary of Superstitions.* New York: Oxford University Press, 1989.

Palaiseul, Jean. *Grandmother's Secrets.* New York: G. P. Putnam's Sons, 1974.

Paulsen, Kathryn. *The Complete Book of Magic & WitchCraft.* New York: Signet Books, 1970.

Plat, Hugh. *Delights for Ladies.* London: Hvmfrey Lownes, 1602.

Roberts, Annie Lise. *Cornucopia: The Lore of Fruits and Vegitables.* New York: Knickerbocker Press, 1998.

Ryall, Rhiannon. *West Country Wicca.* Custer, WA: Phoenix Publishing, 1989.

Schapira, Joel, David and Karl. *The Book of Coffee and Tea.* New York: St. Martins Press, 1906.

Singer, Charles J.. *Early English Magic and Medicine.* London: British Academy, 1920.

Skinner, Charles M. *Myths and Legends of Flowers, Trees, Fruits and Plants.* Philadelphia: Lippincott, 1925.

Tannahill, Reay. *Food in History.* New York: Three Rivers Press, 1998.

Tchudi, Stephen N. *Soda Poppery.* New York: Charles Scribner Sons, 1942.

Telesco, Patricia. *Folkways.* St. Paul, MN: Llewellyn Publications, 1994.

_____. *Magick Made Easy.* San Francisco: Harper Collins San Francisco, 1999.

_____. *A Victorian Flower Oracle.* St. Paul, MN: Llewellyn Publications, 1994.

_____. *A Victorian Grimoire.* St. Paul, MN: Llewellyn Publications, 1992.

Tillona, P. *Feast of Flowers.* New York: Funk & Wagnall, 1969.

Turgeon, Charlotte. ed., *Encyclopedia of Creative Cooking.* New York: Weathervane Press, 1982.

Turner, B. C. A. *Fruit Wines.* London: Mills & Boon LTD, 1973.

Urdag, Geore. *The Squib Ancient Pharmacy.* New York: Squibb and Sons, 1940.

Walker, Barbara. *Womens Dictionary of Sacred Symbols and Objects.* San Francisco: Harper Row, 1988.

Websters Universal Unabridged Dictionary. New York: World Syndicate Publishing, 1937.

Wheelwrite, Edith Grey. *Medicinal Plant and Their History.* New York: Dover Publications, 1974.

Whiteside, Lorraine. *Fresh Fruit Drinks.* New York Thorsons Publishers, 1984.

Williams, Judith. *Judes Home Herbal.* St. Paul, MN: Llewellyn Publications, 1992.

Woodward, Nancy Hyden. *Teas of the World.* New York: Macmillan Publishing Company, 1980.

Younger, William. *Gods, Men & Wine.* Cleveland, OH: World Publishing, 1966.

INDEX

Index